IN FRANCE

Written and edited by

Pat McLagan, B.A.

Spencer Thomas, B.A., Ph.D. (Geography)
Roger Morel, L.ès L. (History)
Helen Doughty, B.A., Cert. Ed.
Barbara Hopper, B.A., Cert. Ed.

Cartoons by
David Lock

Illustrations by

NELSON   *Chancerel*

Introduction

At last someone has had the courage to do it. Complete with visual aid (a humorous line drawing) and a multiple choice of answers the writers of In France have revealed the mysteries of the 'bidet'. The information is to be found in a section dealing with 'some very small differences' between British and French houses and hotels and will I am sure be most welcome to many a puzzled first time visitor to France.

The stated aim of In France is to provide school pupils learning French with project material to be used before, during and after an educational visit to France. The writers pack into its 96 pages a well illustrated gold mine of information for the young visitor to France and, I dare say, it has much to offer the more seasoned traveller with its up to date facts and figures.

In France has obviously been written by people who like France and the French and who know the country very well. Besides the linguists the team of authors includes a geographer and a historian and some excellent illustrators with a good sense of humour. Their book should help to dispel some of the prejudices we in this country are so adept at passing on to our children about our nearest if not always our dearest neighbours across the Channel.

School visits to France can do much for the education of young people. They can also do harm to both the young visitor and to his hosts if inadequately prepared. This book will serve as a most useful aid to the teacher who is making a serious attempt to maximise for his pupils the benefits of educational visits to France, besides providing entertaining support material for French studies in the classroom.

Paddy Carpenter
January 1981
The Central Bureau for Educational Visits
and Exchanges, Dorset St., London, W1

Photographs

The French Government Tourist Office 12, 13, 15, 19, 21, 28, 34, 37, 41, 44, 45, 57, 58, 59, 60, 61, 62, 63, 64, 65, 66, 67, 69, 71, 72, 73, 76, 78, 79
Documentation Française 6 (photo Elysée), 26, 37, 64 (Interphotothèque, Sodel-Brigaud), 68 (Richard) (Interphotothèque), 70 (Holzapfel), 71, 72 (Elysée), 76 (parlement Européen), 77 (Rigal), (CRDP, Clermont-Ferrand)
Duncan Prowse 12, 13, 19, 23, 25, 31, 38, 44, 49, 54, 57, 78, 85, 89
Graeme McLagan 25, 32, 38, 39, 45, 46, 84
Dr Spencer Thomas 10, 12, 13, 21, 27, 34, 35, 38, 57

SIRP-PTT 32, 33, 44, 54
Food and Wine from France 17, 22, 43, 48
Sopexa 16, 17, 48, 63, 65, 76, 85
Etamic Ltd., 48
Ministère de l'Intérieur (Police Nationale) 44, 83
La Gendarmerie Nationale 44
The French Embassy, London 34, 35
Chorus 10, 83
Camera Press 74, 75
Snark International 73
RATP 46, 47, 86, 87
BBC photo library 61
Marks and Spencer Ltd. 21
Janine Wiedel 50

French Railways, London 10, 27
SNCF, Paris 10
Citroën 34, 46
La Caisse Nationale des Monuments Historiques et des Sites (Arch. Phot. Paris S.P.A.D.E.M.) 62, 66, 75
The British Film Institute 36
Normandy Ferries 10
Harrison and Laking (money photography) 24, 91
Organisation des Foires de Champagne 63

Astérix, p. 58, by Goscinny and Uderzo reproduced by kind permission of Hodder Dargaud.

We would like to thank the **Michelin Tyre Company** for their contributions of Bibendum drawings for In France. The map on page 83 is from the Michelin Atlas des Grandes Routes no 915, and is reproduced by kind permission of Michelin, France.

Every effort has been made to trace all the copyright holders but the publishers will be pleased to make the necessary arrangements at the first opportunity if there are any omissions.

Chancerel Publishers Ltd.
40, Tavistock Street,
London, WC2E 7PB

Thomas Nelson & Sons Ltd.
Nelson House,
Mayfield Road,
Walton on Thames,
Surrey KT12 5PL

ISBN 0 17 439081 5
NCN 3319/27 0
This edition published by Thomas Nelson and Sons Ltd.

Monographic origination by ReproSharp, London EC1,
Colour by La Comolito, Milan.
Printed in Italy.

About the authors

Pat McLagan is a former Advisory Teacher to the Inner London Education Authority. This work involved production of language teaching materials as well as in-service training of teachers. She has taught French to pupils of all abilities in Newcastle-on-Tyne and Inner London.

Dr Spencer Thomas is Head of the Department of Geography at the West Sussex Institute of Higher Education.

M. Roger Morel teaches history at the Lycée Français de Londres.

Contents

We are the Légourd family and we're here to help you get to know our country – before, during and after your visit. We live in Étretat, in Normandy, right by the sea.

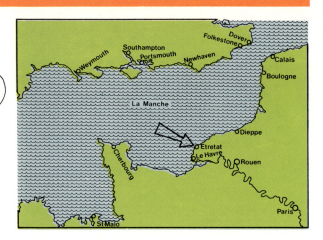

Bonjour! Je m'appelle Gérard Légourd.

Bonjour! Je m'appelle Dominique Légourd

Salut! Je m'appelle Michel!

Salut! Je m'appelle Claire!

Now is the time to start thinking about your trip to France. We hope that IN FRANCE will help you make the most of it. We're going to try to prepare you for your visit – giving you lots of things to do before you leave; telling you what to look out for when you're there; and showing you how much you've learned about France once you're back.

To start you off, let me give you a few hints on what you should and shouldn't do in France. Every country has its own ways of doing things and it's a good idea to try and fit in with them.

C'est très bon!

DO look to the **left** before stepping off the pavement. Cars drive on the right in France and they do not stop for pedestrians.

DON'T forget to carry the address of your hotel on a piece of paper. You can show it to someone if you get lost.

DO be sure to comment favourably on the meal at the hotel. The French take a great pride in their cooking.

Your book is split up into:

Getting ready
Pages 4-37

So that you're really well prepared, try to do all of **Getting ready** *before* you leave for France.

On the spot
Pages 38-55

The **On the spot** pages have to be completed *during* your stay of course. They have darker edges so that you can find them easily.

Now you're back!
Pages 80-96

The **Now you're back** section helps you to relive parts of your stay. Do these pages when you return.

France – Region by Region Pages 56-79

This section will interest you before, during *and* after your visit, especially the section describing *your* region.

DO try dipping your bread and butter into your breakfast coffee or hot chocolate as the French do.

Do say **merci** when you want to say **No**, thank-you. Often you needn't bother saying the **Non**.

DO remember to ask for **un café au lait** or **un thé au lait** if you want your coffee or tea with milk, otherwise you will get it black.

DO say Pardon, Monsieur, Madame or **Mademoiselle** if you accidentally bump into someone.

DON'T turn a tap marked C and expect cold water to come from it. Remember:
C = chaud
F = froid

DO shake hands when you are introduced to a French person.

DO try to speak as much French as possible. Don't cheat by pointing!

Quiz?? Quiz?? Quiz?? Quiz??

See how many of these you can do without looking up the answers!

1 What are the colours of the French flag?
a. red green white ☐
b. red orange black ☐
c. blue white red ☐

2 What is the name of the supersonic passenger aeroplane made jointly by the French and English?
a. Concorde ☐
b. Caravelle ☐
c. Concarneau ☐

3 What sort of food is Camembert?
a. ham ☐
b. fruit ☐
c. cheese ☐

4 Who is the President of France?
a. M. Giscard d'Estaing ☐
b. M. Pompidou ☐
c. Charles de Gaulle ☐

5 What is the Paris underground system called?
a. U-bahn ☐
b. Métro ☐
c. Météo ☐

6 Where would you see the letters SNCF?
a. on a church ☐
b. at a post office ☐
c. at a railway station ☐

7 What do the names Dior, Yves St Laurent and Chanel remind you of?
a. Seaways ☐
b. Food ☐
c. Fashion ☐

8 A famous cycle race is held every year in France. It is called
a. Le Tour de force ☐
b. Le Tour de France ☐
c. Les 24 heures du Mans ☐

9 Which of these are the names of French mineral waters?
a. Vittel ☐
b. Evian ☐
c. Orangina ☐
d. Perrier ☐
e. Malvern ☐

10 What is the name of the famous French tyre company?
a. Pirelli ☐
b. Firestone ☐
c. Michelin ☐

11 Which of these things can you do in a **bureau de change?**
a. Buy stamps ☐
b. Change your clothes ☐
c. Change money ☐

12 What is the French name for the English Channel?
a. Le chenal français ☐
b. La mer Anglo-Normande ☐
c. La Manche ☐

13 What is the longest river in France? It's famous for many beautiful châteaux
a. Seine ☐
b. Loire ☐
c. Garonne ☐

14 Is Jean-Paul Belmondo famous for his
a. Politics ☐
b. Books ☐
c. Films ☐

15 Who was the French soldier burned to death at the stake in 1431?
a. General Leclerc ☐
b. Joan of Arc ☐
c. Marie Antoinette ☐

16 Which mountains form a border between France, Switzerland and Italy?
a. The Alps ☐
b. The Pyrenees ☐
c. The Jura ☐

(Answers on page 96)

Extra! Extra! Extra! Extra!

Some even harder questions! See if you can find the answers to all of them by doing a little research!

☆ Name the two international airports in Paris.

☆ What is the town of **Lourdes** in South West France famous for?

☆ Who was the first person to fly across the English Channel?

☆ Where might you see PAR AVION written?

☆ Louis Pasteur made a wonderful scientific discovery in the last century. What was it?

☆ Name two dishes you associate with the French.

☆ Name the French national anthem. It has close associations with a large port in the south of France. You can find the words on page 96.

☆ Name one famous French painter and one famous French writer.

Comparing the Languages

Notice how many of them have something to do with cooking! Say them first with an English accent then with a very French one!
Ask the meanings of those you don't know.

"I'm going to get you to say something in French now! You probably use quite a few French words in English."

gâteau
cuisine
chalet
souvenir

rendez-vous
cordon bleu
pâtisserie
soufflé
pâté
à la carte
à la mode
mousse
pas de deux
quiche
purée
meringue

carte blanche
caramel
tour de force
tête-à-tête
ballet
hors d'oeuvre
bouquet garni
sauté
joie de vivre
R.S.V.P. (Répondez, s'il vous plaît)
coup de grâce

The French have also borrowed a lot of English and American words. Here's a list of English words which we use in France. We pronounce them differently, of course. Try saying them with a really strong French accent! If you hear or see any others when you're in France, add them to the list.

Notice that they are all 'le' words!

le cowboy
le ticket
le footing
le pull-over
le pyjama
le camping
le bowling
le babysitter
le sport
le self-service
le bulldozer
le talc
le clown
le basketball
le club
le zigzag
le juke-box
le dancing

le weekend
le sandwich
le hot-dog
le hit-parade
le steak
le shampooing
l'interview
les chips (potato crisps)
le football

Speak up!
Words you can't do without!

Je ne comprends pas.
Merci
Je m'appelle . . . . .
Au revoir

Bonsoir
Pardon
C'est très bon
C'est combien?

BONJOUR, MADEMOISELLE!

EUH... BONJOUR, MADAME!

BONJOUR, MONSIEUR!

Ça va? Ah, oui! Ça va bien!

Ah, non! Ça ne va pas!

Many other words are similar in both languages. I'm sure you'll be able to add to this list...
la musique, le cinéma, le zoo, le détective, le dîner, délicieux, le train, le buffet, la cigarette, le collège, l'enfant, la couleur, le supermarché, la salade, la crème, l'hôpital, le film, la carrotte, le dentiste, l'appartement, la télévision, la radio, le café, le restaurant, le garage, super, la tomate, ordinaire, les raisins...

7

On the road

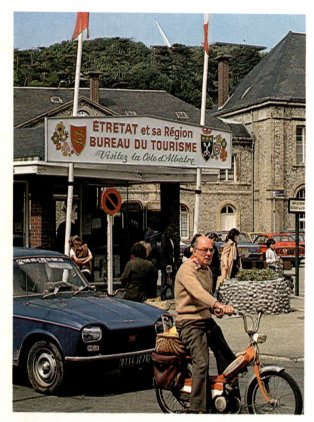

> Here's a photo of our local tourist office in Etretat. A tourist office is often called un Syndicat d'Initiative.

Before you set off you'd probably like to have a look at the sort of area you'll be staying in! Find out what it will be like by writing to the local tourist office for information.

Our Syndicats are excellent! Provided you don't arrive at lunch-time — almost everything shuts between 12 and 2 — you will be provided with brochures, maps and information about your area . . . and all free.

Miss A. Knight,
7, Piper Road,
BOLTON,
Lancashire,
ANGLETERRE

Bolton, le 3 mars 19..
Syndicat d'Initiative,
7690 ETRETAT,
FRANCE

Monsieur, Je voudrais passer des vacances avec un groupe scolaire à Etretat du 1 au 15 août. Je vous prie de bien vouloir m'envoyer les renseignements suivants:
un plan de la ville d'Etretat
des brochures sur la région
des informations sur des évènements
sportifs et culturels au mois d'août.

Avec mes remerciements,

A Knight

Where will you be staying?

1 Mark on this map the name of the place where you'll be staying.
2 Put in PARIS and the French Channel port you will land at.
3 Trace your route from the Channel coast as far as you can.
4 Find out the name of the *province* you will be in. Look at the map on page 56 for help.
5 In which *département* will you be staying? Find out from the map on page 39.
6 Draw in the nearest rivers and mountains. The map on page 12 may help.

7 Put in the names of the countries which border on France.

The time in France is generally one hour *ahead* of British time.
French summer time (L'Heure d'été) lasts from April to October.

What will the weather be like?

The weather in northern France is similar to that in southern Britain. In the south of France you can expect temperatures to be much higher than those in most of Britain, with quite a bit more sunshine. But when it rains, it really pours! This weather forecast is for a day in June.

1 What is the highest temperature expected in the Paris area?
2 What will the weather be like in Brittany today?
3 Is rain expected in Provence?
4 Will I need a raincoat in Reims?
5 In which areas is fog expected?
6 Which area will expect the finest, hottest weather?
7 Judging from this map, what sort of weather would you expect in southern England on

Le temps pour jeudi, 19 juin

Beau temps
Temps couvert
Brouillard
Averse

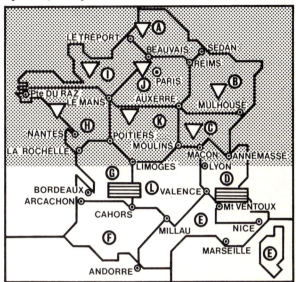

Températures prévues

A	de 9	à	18
B	de 8	à	15
C	de 8	à	16
D	de 15	à	23
E	de 12	à	22
F	de 15	à	23
G	de 10	à	21
H	de 11	à	18
I	de 10	à	19
J	de 9	à	19
K	de 9	à	18
L	de 9	à	20

this particular day?
8 The temperatures are all in degrees centigrade. What is freezing point in centigrade?

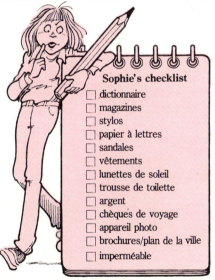

Sophie has been doing her packing. She's checking to make sure that she hasn't forgotten anything. Is there anything missing? Tick off the items for her as you see them on the bed. Then put in the things she's forgotten.

Sophie's checklist
- dictionnaire
- magazines
- stylos
- papier à lettres
- sandales
- vêtements
- lunettes de soleil
- trousse de toilette
- argent
- chèques de voyage
- appareil photo
- brochures/plan de la ville
- imperméable

Extra Extra Extra Extra Extra Extra Extra Extra Extra Extra

**** Find out how many possible methods there are of crossing the Channel.
**** How many different sea routes are there?
**** Petrol is sold in litres in France. Find out how many litres there are to a gallon.
**** Write down what you think would be the advantages of a Channel tunnel. Consider costs, time, international relations, pleasure.
**** Ask your friends, family and teachers for their impressions of France. It may remind older people of the war. Some may think immediately of food! Write down 5 different impressions in 5 sentences.

Getting there

How are **you** going to get to France? These photographs show a number of ways of moving people and goods.

Various forms of transport are shown in the pictures.

Which is the quickest?

Which is the slowest?

Which is the oldest form of transportation?

Which is the most modern?

1 Which of these methods of transport will you use to reach your destination in France?

2 If you had the choice, which means of transport would you use to travel from:
your home to the local library?
London to Paris?
Newcastle-on-Tyne to Nice?
a village to the nearest town?
And which would you use to transport oil from Marseilles to Paris?

3 What factors influence your choice of transport under different circumstances?

A Schools Abroad coach

Unloading a barge

Oxen power

A cross Channel ferry

A French Rail hovercraft

A French trolley bus

Cars at Versailles

A Renault lorry

An S.N.C.F. train

Les autoroutes

We give our motorways names as well as numbers. Find out what the names mean.

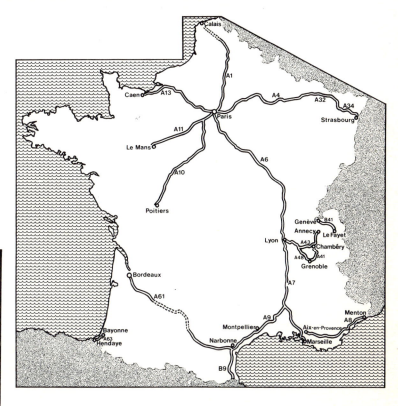

Then look at the map and see if the names fit the areas they are in. Other countries, such as Italy, name their motorways too. Why do you think they do this?

A1	Autoroute du Nord
A13	Autoroute de Normandie
A4 A32 A34	Autoroute de L'Est
A6 A7	Autoroute du Soleil
A10	L'Aquitaine
A41 A43 A48	Autoroutes Alpines
A11	L'Océane
B41	Autoroute Blanche
A63	Autoroute de La Côte Basque
A8	La Provençale
A9	La Languedocienne
B9	La Catalane
A61	Autoroute des 2 Mers

Imagine that there is to be a competition to find the best names for the *British* motorways. What do you think would be the most suitable names for the M1, M2, M3, M4, M5, M6, M62, M9 and M11?

Which route to take?

The two cities, marked on the diagram A and B, are joined by three different routes. You could travel by *river*, by *rail* or by *motorway*.

If you look at the routes from the air they would look just as they do on the diagram.

1 Which is the shortest, most direct route?
2 Which is the longest, most devious route?
3 Why are some routes straighter than others?
4 Name two ways of 'straightening' the routes.
5 Why bother to iron out the curves?
6 Is the shortest route necessarily the quickest? Why?
7 Describe the route you will take on your school journey.

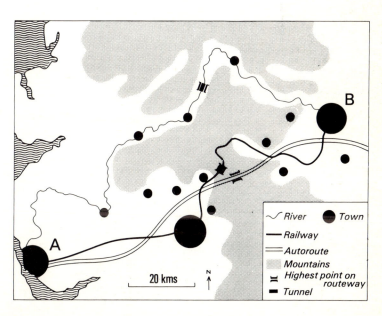

Studying the landscape

France is a big country. —about 4½ times the size of England! As you travel around you'll probably pass through a very wide variety of scenery and landscapes.

The photographs on these pages show just a few of the landscapes which make up France.

Look carefully at the photos and work out . . .

1 Which are the highest areas?
2 Which are the flattest areas?
3 Which are the major river valleys?
4 What is the name of the river valley nearest your destination?
5 What are the names of the rivers you will cross, and the hills and mountains you will pass on your school journey?
6 Which area was once upon a time a series of volcanoes? How can you tell? Why are they no longer active?

Put in the names of the main mountainous areas and rivers.

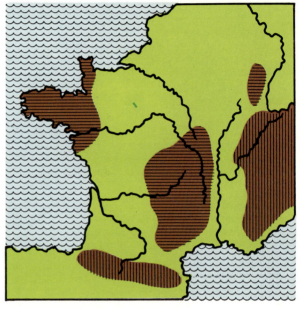

Alps   Vosges   Jura   Pyrenees
Central Massif   Armorican Massif
Loire   Seine   Saône   Rhône   Rhine
Dordogne   Garonne

Above: *The river Lot meanders through vineyards*

Below: *Alpe d'Huez, Isère*

Right: *St-Cirq-Lapopie, Lot*

Above: *Le Puy*

Below: *Village perché — Vaucluse*

Right: *Rocamadour, Lot*

What sort of scenery do you prefer? France offers a very wide variety, but the countryside is not composed of 'natural' landscapes alone.

Is it really natural?

There are many man-made features in the landscape, some of which enhance its beauty and some of which take away from it.

Some parts of the countryside are more popular and are therefore overrun with people.

Others are remote and peaceful.

Unfortunately the countryside is not able to provide a living for everyone who wants to live there and many people move to towns. The consequences of this can be seen in many places with dilapidated houses and abandoned land. Attempts are being made to revitalise rural areas by attracting tourists.

Above left: *Crowded beach, La Baule*
Left: *Derelict cottages, Brittany*
Above: *La Grande Motte, new tourist development in Languedoc*
Right: *Le Pont du Gard, Roman aqueduct*

1 Make a list of man-made features which add to the beauty of the scenery.
   Then list the man-made features which detract from the scenery.
2 Which parts of the countryside become saturated with visitors? The crowded areas are sometimes called 'gluepots'. Why?
3 Give as many reasons as possible why people move from rural areas to urban areas.
4 Try and identify as many ways as possible in which people are being persuaded to spend their holidays in the countryside. Design a poster attracting people to a remote village in France.

13

Settling in!

Let me show you around the sort of rooms you may have when you're IN FRANCE. The drawing shows a bedroom in a French hotel. Try to learn as many names as you can before you leave. You may need to ask the hotel staff about them when you're ON THE SPOT in France.

Key					
1 le lit	5 le traversin	10 la serrure	15 la baignoire	20 la serviette
2 la housse	6 le cintre	11 la clef	16 la douche	21 le bidet
3 le drap	7 la lampe	12 la fenêtre	17 le WC	22 le papier toilette
4 la couverture	8 le téléphone	13 les rideaux	18 le lavabo	
	9 la porte	14 les volets	19 les robinets	

Finding your way in the hotel

Imagine you are at the hotel. Practise asking for these things with a partner.

Example: *Où est l'ascenseur, s'il vous plaît?*

1 la salle à manger   2 le WC   3 la salle de bains   4 la clef numéro trente   5 Où sont mes copains?!

Just in case . . . things don't work!

Example: *La vidange ne fonctionne pas*

Now say the same about these things.

Sophie's checklist

Write to the French Government Tourist Office asking for a list of hotels in your town.
Pinpoint where you'll be staying on a plan of the town.
Write your name, address and telephone number in France on a small card.
It may be useful to keep this with you in case you get lost. Give a copy to your parents too.

Extra Extra Extra Extra

☆☆☆☆ **Find out** which code you would use to telephone your hotel from Britain.

☆☆☆☆ **Design** a poster in English attracting British tourists to a 2 star hotel in Etretat, France.

☆☆☆☆ **What** do you need from a hotel?
Write down five ways in which a 4 star hotel could differ from a 1 star hotel. Would it be worth paying the extra for the 4 star?

You can stay in the grand luxe of a **Relais et Châteaux** Hotel or in simpler style in a **Logis de France.** French hotels spread the whole range. Tourist hotels do have their prices fixed by the comité départemental de tourisme. On the back of your bedroom door you'll see a notice giving prices of rooms in the hotel.

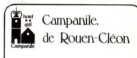

Meals at the hotel

Hotels with restaurants will expect you to take your evening meal there. If you stay more than a few nights you will then be on a demi-pension rate for bed and evening meal. Breakfast is often charged separately and need not be taken at the hotel.

The first French meal you have may well be breakfast! **(le petit déjeuner)** It's often served in your room! Don't expect breakfast cereals, orange juice or bacon and egg. Delicious French bread or croissants, butter, jam, milky coffee, tea or hot chocolate are usual.

You may be asked if you would like:
Un café au lait complet
Un thé au lait complet
or **Un chocolat complet**

There may be a notice on the back of your bedroom door giving times of meals.

> Petit déjeuner
>   de 7h à 10h
> Déjeuner
>   de 12h à 14h
> Dîner
>   de 19h à 21h

Things you'll find inside a French house or hotel will be much the same as things in your house. But you may notice some very small differences...

A long bolster on a bed instead of a pillow
Shutters at the windows, so no need for thick curtains.
Fasteners so shutters don't blow open and bang!

Different types of lavatory flush – you lift the knob on this one.
Window locks consisting of a rod passing down through the middle of a double window.
No chain on the plug! Don't try to take it out! Lift or lower the plug using the lever between the taps.

Showers are more popular in France.

But drains aren't always so efficient. So be careful not to block plug holes!

I don't think that's what it's for, Justin!

A bidet is
a. for washing clothes in ☐
b. for washing your bottom ☐
c. a French lavatory ☐
d. for pets to drink from ☐

Bon Appétit!

Did you know that some people go to France just for the food?

Even the most fervently anti-French must admit that this is one area in which the French excel! Our **cuisine** is said to be the best in the world!

The types of foods you will get in France will not be much different from those you get at home. But there will be *one* difference – your food in France will be prepared, cooked and served in a much, much better way!

Quiche Lorraine

Un menu à prix fixe

A word you will see again and again on menus like this is

Ou = Or

(see page 43 for a mini menu translator!)

Menu à 50F

Hors d'oeuvre

Oeuf mayonnaise
ou
Crudités
ou
Pâté Maison
ou
Salade Niçoise

Entrées

Steak garni
ou
Filet de sole
ou
Côte de porc

Salade

Plateau de fromages

Dessert

Pâtisserie ou Glace ou Fruit

Boisson en sus   Service compris

Practise asking for things from this menu with a partner. Be the waiter, then swap roles and be 'he customer.

Vous avez choisi, mademoiselle?

Euh...oui. Le menu à 40 francs, s'il vous plaît. Je voudrais une salade de tomate, du pâté, une côte de porc...

Je voudrais des crudités, s'il vous plaît.
Et comme boisson?
De l'eau, s'il vous plaît.
Une demi-bouteille d'Évian, s'il vous plaît.
Je voudrais une pâtisserie, s'il vous plaît.
Pour moi, le filet de sole.
Et je voudrais une glace à la fraise.
Qu'est-ce que vous voulez comme dessert?
Vous voulez du fromage?
C'est bon?
J'aime le pâté. C'est bon!

Extra Extra Extra

**** Give yourself a taste of French food before you get there! Make a French salad sauce. You need
3 tablespoons OIL
1 tablespoon VINEGAR
Pinch SALT
Little PEPPER
Little MUSTARD
Mix all ingredients well till the mixture is cloudy and smooth. Add to lettuce and HEY PRESTO you have a French *salade*. Add to sliced tomatoes, cucumber, grated carrot or grated red cabbage and you have *des crudités*! It's nothing like British salad cream!

**** Name 5 famous French dishes. Try and find a recipe for 1 of them. Look in cookery books in the library.

**** N.B. DON'T buy sweets in France! They are more expensive. If you are really HOOKED on them, take them with you from home.

NB. Things like frogs' legs and snails are not our everyday foods – they are very much specialities!

Here are some of the things which have made French food world famous.

Charcuterie

Escargots de Bourgogne

Above Crudités   Below Fromages

Charcuterie
Pâté
Pâté is made from pork, eggs and milk. There are 2 sorts – rough, coarse pâté like *pâté de campagne,* and smooth pâté like *pâté de foie.* Smooth pâtés usually have chicken or pork liver added. Pâtés are also made with duck, turkey, chicken. Pâté can also be bought in tins.
Jambon
You can buy cooked ham, like *jambon de Paris,* or cured ham, *jambon cru.* Cured ham has spices and salt rubbed into it and is then left to cure for several months. You'll find many different sorts of ham in France, including *jambon blanc . . .* and *jambon d'York!*
Saucisson
Saucissons are either cooked or dried (*sec*). French garlic sausage (*saucisson à l'ail*) is cooked. *Saucisson sec* is harder than cooked saucisson. Both are eaten straight from the *charcuterie* without further cooking.

Fromages
There are several hundred different varieties of French cheese, made from cow's, goat's or ewe's milk. Try as many as you can when you're in France. Ask for *cinquante grammes* and you'll get a piece small enough for you and your friends to taste.
French cheese is either:
Soft cheese with white rind which you can eat
Camembert, Brie, Carré de L'Est
Soft cheese with brine-washed rind, golden in colour. These have a stronger taste
Livarot, Pont L'Évêque
Hard cheese shaped like large wheels
Emmental, Comté
Semi-hard cheese, pressed but uncooked
Saint Paulin, Tomme de Savoie
Blue-veined cheeses
Bleu d'Auvergne, Bleu de Bresse
Processed cheese
Cheese spreads, Walnut or grape cheese

Around the town

Let me show you around town. Then you can practise on your own before you go. For a plan of your French town, write to the Syndicat d'Initiative.

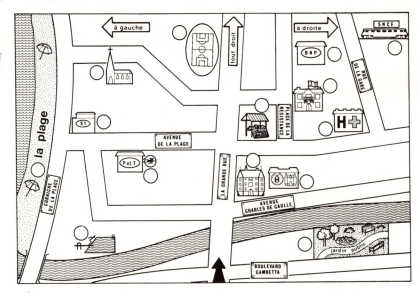

It's difficult to tell what's what at first – the signs and symbols look so foreign. See if you can decipher them.

The principal landmarks have been drawn as symbols, but the numbers which should go in the circles next to the places, haven't been put in yet. Match the symbols with the names on the **légende**. Then *write the numbers in the empty circles*.

LÉGENDE		
1 La gare	5 La mairie	10 L'Hôtel du Château
2 L'hôpital	6 La banque	11 La piscine
3 Le Syndicat d'Initiative	7 La poste	12 Le marché
4 La plage	8 Le stade	13 L'église
	9 Le château	14 Le jardin public

Work out where these people want to go to.

1 Ask your way to 10 of the places on the plan.
Example:
La poste, s'il vous plaît?

2 Point to each place on the plan. Say it's name. Say if it is à gauche, à droite or tout droit.

3 With a partner, ask your way to 8 places on the plan. Your partner tells you which way to go. Try to use as much French as possible. Use the conversations on this page as a guide.

Le — —, s'il vous plaît?

Tournez à droite au Boulevard Gambetta, et c'est à votre gauche.

Pour aller à la —, s'il vous plaît?

Vous prenez la deuxième rue à gauche, c'est l'Avenue de la Plage, et vous continuez tout droit, tout droit, tout droit.

Le —, s'il vous plaît?

Allez tout droit. Traversez le pont, puis c'est à votre droite. C'est au coin de la Grande Rue et de l'Avenue Charles de Gaulle.

La —, s'il vous plaît?

Continuez tout droit, puis prenez la troisième rue sur votre droite, et c'est juste en face. C'est tout près du marché sur la Place de la Résistance.

Et où es-tu maintenant?   A game to play in pairs.
Think of a place on the plan. Without revealing your destination, give directions to your partner to the place, starting from the arrow. Finish your list of directions by saying: Et où es-tu maintenant?   Then reverse roles.

These photos show you different buildings and places around the town.
Unfortunately, we have forgotten to match the texts with the photos they describe. Which texts go with the photos? Write the appropriate letters in the boxes next to the photos.

A Any large country house or stately home in France is called **un château**. You'll probably see several châteaux on your visit. Unlike castles in Britain, French châteaux were not always built primarily for defence purposes. French royalty and aristocrats used to have houses in Paris as well as châteaux in the country. The most famous châteaux are in the beautiful country setting of the valley of the Loire, the longest river in France. This one is the Château d'Ussé.

B Come here to buy stamps, send a telegram or telephone. For your stamps head for the counter marked **affranchissements** or **timbres.** In Paris some post offices are open 24 hours a day, but most will keep office hours and close for two hours at lunch time. Look out for pedestrian crossings like the one in the photo. It has an illuminated sign telling **piétons** when they can cross. Often the sign will say **piétons – arrêtez** or **piétons – passez.** Is the road to **Saint-Claude** a major trunk road?

C This garage or station-service is

near another important building in the town. Which is it?

D The windows above this bank are typically French with their shutters and little wrought-iron balconies. Banks are usually open from 9am – 12 noon and from 2pm – 4pm. They are closed either on Mondays or Saturdays and always on Sundays.

E A town hall can be called **une mairie** or **un hôtel de ville.** As the name suggests hôtels de ville are more usual in larger towns. The town hall houses offices of the mayor, the receveur who receives local taxes, social security, records of sales and purchases of land, records of births, deaths and marriages, and sometimes the Syndicat d'Initiative. Civil wedding ceremonies take place here before the religious ceremony in church.

Sophie's checklist

Take note of your surroundings in your home town. Look carefully at the things below as you see them around the streets. When you're **On the spot in France** compare them to their French equivalents. Notice – colour, shape, size, style, lettering, numbers

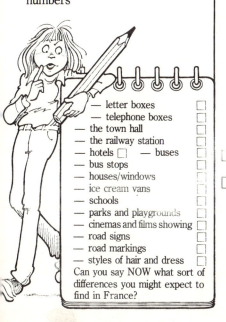

- letter boxes ☐
- telephone boxes ☐
- the town hall ☐
- the railway station ☐
- hotels ☐ – buses ☐
- bus stops ☐
- houses/windows ☐
- ice cream vans ☐
- schools ☐
- parks and playgrounds ☐
- cinemas and films showing ☐
- road signs ☐
- road markings ☐
- styles of hair and dress ☐

Can you say NOW what sort of differences you might expect to find in France?

Cities, Towns and Villages

Are you going to stay in a city, a town, or a village?

In France, as in most countries, the settlements form a pyramid.

The diagram shows the largest city, the capital, Paris, at the top.

The isolated farms, being the smallest settlements, are at the bottom of the pyramid.

How big is the place you'll be staying in in France? How will it fit into this pyramid?

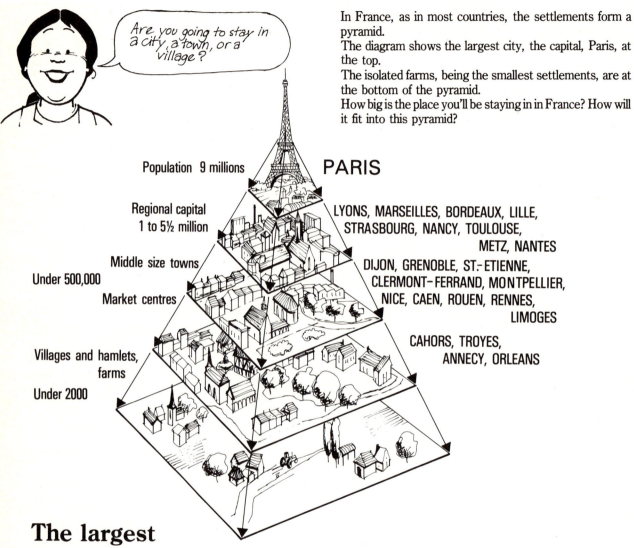

Population 9 millions — **PARIS**

Regional capital 1 to 5½ million — LYONS, MARSEILLES, BORDEAUX, LILLE, STRASBOURG, NANCY, TOULOUSE, METZ, NANTES

Middle size towns

Under 500,000 — DIJON, GRENOBLE, ST.-ETIENNE, CLERMONT–FERRAND, MONTPELLIER, NICE, CAEN, ROUEN, RENNES, LIMOGES

Market centres — CAHORS, TROYES, ANNECY, ORLEANS

Villages and hamlets, farms

Under 2000

The largest

The largest city, Paris, possesses certain facilities and amenities which other cities do not have because their population is not large enough.

For example, Paris has famous art galleries, such as The Louvre, cultural centres such as the Pompidou Centre, sports centres such as the Parc des Princes, the leading theatres and fashion houses and so on.

It also has the largest and most famous shops with names like Galeries Lafayette and one which you might recognise – Marks and Spencer! These act like magnets attracting people from all over France to spend their time and money in the centre of Paris.

The next layer of cities are the regional capitals such as Strasbourg.

They have fewer facilities, perhaps one theatre, a museum, branches of the main department stores, because fewer people live in and around these cities.

The middle size and market towns have even lower populations and fewer facilities.

By the time you arrive at the villages there may only be one or two shops such as a **boulangerie** (bread shop) and an **épicerie** (general grocer's).

Marks and Spencer, Boulevard Haussmann, Paris

Le Centre Georges Pompidou, Paris

Strasbourg, new housing and shops

The Louvre, Paris — Vénus de Milo

Market day at Millau, Languedoc

A peaceful village

When you have received a plan of your town and information about it from the Syndicat d'Initiative, try these questions:

1 What is the name of your nearest town or village in France?

2 What is the population of the nearest town or village?

3 What facilities and amenities does it have? If it is a village name the types of shops and organisations. If it is a town or city list the different types of shops, the services such as libraries and hospitals, the provision for entertainment and leisure.

4 If the settlement nearest you does not have a large range of goods and services, where do the inhabitants go to get them? For example, if it is a village, where is the nearest doctor or optician?

5 Why do some settlements become more important than others?

6 Is there any evidence that the settlement nearest you or those you will visit are any more or less important than they were in the past? For instance, does it have a market place but no longer has a market?

7 Why do branches of the same shops have different floor areas and different lengths of frontage in different places?

8 What place in Britain has a similar range of facilities and amenities as Paris? Answer the same question for other countries such as Germany and Australia. Is it always the capital city which possesses the greatest range? Why? How do you think capital cities evolved?

Mais...où est le marché?

Signs and adverts

There are some signs in France which you've just got to understand. Look at these cartoons and you'll see what I mean!

You'll need to know when things are not allowed. There are two ways of saying YOU MUST NOT...

1 Il est **Interdit de**...
2 Il est **défendu de**
   fumer
   cracher
   marcher sur la pelouse
   stationner...
You'll find lots more **On the spot!**

See if you can spot any adverts for French products, films and books. Look in magazines, newspapers, in the street and on television.

Make a list. Here are some to start you off. Put names to them and tick them off as you find them.

Sophie's checklist
☐ Perfume
☐ Wine
☐ Mineral Water
☐ Books (Astérix, Tintin, Babar)
☐ Cheese
☐ Cars
☐ Clothes
☐ Cigarettes
☐ Fruit
☐ Vegetables
☐ Crockery

What particular types of French goods are popular here?

Information from signs

Granville is in Normandy. The museum there is not open all year round.

Musée du Vieux Granville
Ouvert tous les Jours :
du 1er Jour des Vacances de Printemps
au 1er Dimanche d'Octobre
de 10h. à 12h. et de 14h. à 18h.
Fermé le Mardi

1 When does it close for the winter?
2 When does it open again after the winter?
3 On which day of *every* week is it closed?
4 At what time does it close in the evening?
5 At what time does it re-open after lunch?

1 When can you safely take a walk right along this beach?
2 Try to improve the English translation on this sign!

DIVONNE-LES-BAINS
FÊTE CHAMPÊTRE
AU BORD DU LAC
organisée par les anciens combattants d'Algérie du Comité FNACA de DIVONNE-LES-BAINS

Samedi 5 - Dimanche 6 Juillet

21 h. 30 **GRANDS BALS** Sous CHAPITEAU
avec l'orchestre
«LES CHRYSALIS»
et leur grande formation

Dimanche 6 Juillet

16 h. 00 **CONCERT** donné par la Batterie Fanfare
«LA GESSIENNE et ses MAJORETTES»

18 h. 00 **APÉRITIF Dansant** ENTRÉE LIBRE

Attractions · Côtelettes · Frites · Merguez

BUFFET **BUVETTE**

The poster on the left is advertising a country *fête* in the small town of *Divonne-Les-Bains* near Geneva.

1 Where exactly will the fête take place?
2 What time does the big dance start on Saturday night?
3 What sort of music is there on Sunday afternoon?
4 At 6pm on Sunday night there will be a dance. Why is it called *Un apéritif dansant?*

1 From which part of the *Hôtel Croix Blanche* can you get a good view of the sea?
2 What can you take away from the *Boulangerie/Pâtisserie/Charcuterie?*

5 Name two sorts of food available at the dance.
6 How is the food to be served?

23

money money money money money money

Billets de Banque français

Notes are produced by the Banque de France and must never show any political figures.

Coins, on the other hand, are minted by the State and have République Française and the motto **Liberté, Égalité, Fraternité** on them.

Pièces de Monnaies

Shown on the bank notes are:
500F – Blaise Pascal
100F – Eugène Delacroix (Older notes show Corneille)
50F – Quentin de La Tour (Older notes show Racine)
10F – Hector Berlioz (Older notes show Voltaire)
Some coins have the symbol of the French Republic, *Marianne*, on them. Which are they? Where else might you see *Marianne* and *la semeuse*?

Ça fait combien?

How much money is there in each saucer?
Practise adding up French money. Write the answers in a note book.

 1

 6

 2

 7

 3

 8

 4

 9

 5

 10

Ça fait combien?

How many francs are there to the pound sterling at the moment?
You can find out by going into the nearest bank where you'll see a foreign currency conversion chart.
Before you leave for France, work out a simple conversion card. Write it out in rough first, then transfer it to a piece of card. Carry it with you in France.
Here's an example of a card made when the exchange rate was 9 francs to the pound.

Remember

Check your change. Don't panic if you don't understand the amount of money a shopkeeper or waiter asks you for. Take your time and say:

Répétez plus lentement, s'il vous plaît.

£££FFFF£££FFFF£££FFF

5p = 0.45F	1F = 11p
10p = 0.90F	2F = 22p
15p = 1.35F	3F = 33p
20p = 1.80F	4F = 44p
25p = 2.25F	5F = 55p
50p = 4.50F	6F = 66p
60p = 5.40F	7F = 77p
70p = 6.30F	8F = 88p
80p = 7.20F	9F = £1
90p = 8.10F	10F = £1.11
£1 = 9F	

£££FFFF£££FFFF£££FFF

Let's go shopping

Which shops would you go to for the things on Sophie's list? Try saying the names of the shops.

You can find all the items on Sophie's shopping list somewhere on this page. As you find each one, tick it off.

Then fit the items with the shops which sell them. Write the letter of the appropriate shop next to the item.

Liste

1 un paquet de bonbons ☐
2 une bouteille d'eau
   minérale ☐
3 une baguette ☐
4 un ouvre-bouteille ☐
5 deux tranches de jambon ☐
6 un journal anglais et un
   magazine français ☐
7 un litre de lait ☐
8 des pommes, des oranges
   et des bananes ☐

Extra Extra Extra Extra Extra Extra Extra Extra

Who *are* those famous French men on the banknotes? Look up their names in an encyclopaedia. Write 3 lines about each man.

Are there any famous French *women* who could have been shown on the notes? Remember they must not be politicians, nor must they have any connection with the State.

Is there a difference between the rates of exchange in France and in Britain? Find out from the bank whether it is better to buy your francs here or in France.

Find out if there is a difference between the buying and selling prices of francs. Look in the bank. Write down how much the difference is.

Find out the meaning of the French motto – **Liberté, Égalité, Fraternité**.

Compare the personalities shown on British and French notes and coins. Which designs do you prefer? Which are more colourful?

Inside the city

If you look down on a city from an aeroplane it looks like a giant jig-saw puzzle. On the ground it is difficult to fit the pieces together. If you "cut it in half" like a cake, as in the diagram below, you can recognise distinctive zones or areas.

The photographs on the right show different types of zones or areas.

Not all settlements will have all the zones. It depends on many factors but especially the size and population. The smaller the place the more likely it is that certain zones are missing or less well developed and it is more difficult to pick them out. The larger the place the more likely it is that the pattern of land use is clear.

The central area is usually the most easily recognisable zone. It is nearly always the oldest part containing the market place, the parish church, walls, gates, the town hall and old established industries to remind us of its origins. Nowadays the central area has often been renewed. High buildings of concrete and glass may now house most of the shops, offices and entertainment facilities.

In the zone immediately bordering the central area you usually find the houses of workers who used to work in the city centre. When they were built people used to have to walk to work and so the houses had to be close to the place of work. In Britain they are often in rows of terraces close to each other with small gardens. In France there are almost no individual family houses in the central areas, with most people living in flats.

As public transport became more general and faster, the tram, car, bus and underground have enabled people to live further from the centre and still work there. The growth of suburbs and commuting settlements is a feature of most towns in France and Britain. Perhaps the French are more reluctant to commute than the British as they do like to be able to get home for lunch!

Strasbourg, taken from the air

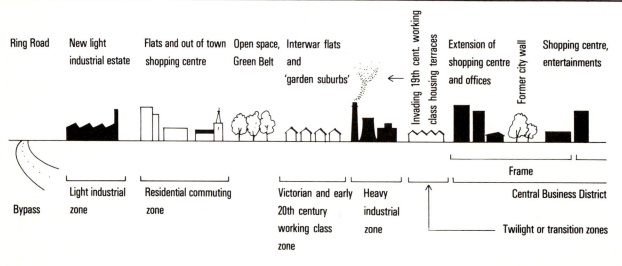

Carrefour hypermarket at Chandlers Ford, England

Thiers, Auvergne

The main street in Pau

A commuter train near Nice.

Answer these questions about the place you live in Britain. Then when you are ON THE SPOT IN FRANCE answer them again, referring to the place you are staying in there.

1 In which part of the settlement are you staying? (Look at the diagram)
2 Which is the oldest part of the settlement near your home?
3 What evidence is there to suggest it is the oldest part?
4 How long does it take to reach the centre from the outskirts by
    (a) walking?
    (b) bus?
    (c) train?
    (d) car?
    Which is quickest? Which is longest?
5 Why do people visit the city centre if it is congested?
6 Why do people choose to live away from most of the amenities and their places of work?
    Why do some people *stay* away?
7 Write down the names of firms/factories/offices near where you live. What do they make?
8 What work do the people living in the villages do? How much of this work is actually in the villages? How many travel to the nearest town to work? Which means of transport do they use?
9 In which part of the city do you find most flats, terraced houses, semi-detached houses and detached houses?
    When you are ON THE SPOT IN FRANCE see if you can **find** any semi-detached houses!

Today many industries and shops have moved out of the inner city areas to the edge of cities or beyond to new industrial estates and parks. They have more space and more attractive surroundings and workers can reach them more easily because they do not have the congestion of the city centre.

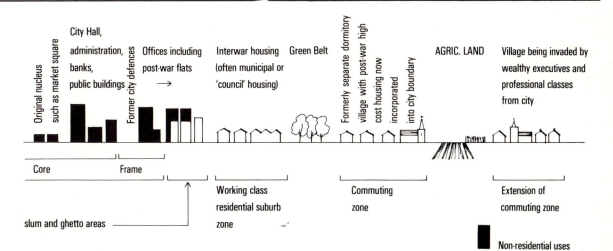

Original nucleus such as market square

City Hall, administration, banks, public buildings

Former city defences

Offices including post-war flats →

Interwar housing (often municipal or 'council' housing)

Green Belt

Formerly separate dormitory village with post-war high cost housing now incorporated into city boundary

AGRIC. LAND

Village being invaded by wealthy executives and professional classes from city

Core   Frame

Working class residential suburb zone

Commuting zone

Extension of commuting zone

slum and ghetto areas

Non-residential uses

At the café

What will you order? Where will you sit? When do you pay? Will you leave a tip?

Even the smallest French village has its café – usually the focal point of village community life – open from early morning till late at night. Even though alcoholic drinks are served, children are allowed to go into cafés provided they don't buy or consume alcohol.

Most cafés have a *terrasse,* a part of the pavement with tables and chairs on it. It's nice to sit outside and watch the world go by, but it's usually cheaper to have a drink standing *au comptoir* (at the bar).

Look at the list of drinks prices – BOISSONS PILOTE – you'll find one in nearly every café. Do study it carefully to work out which drinks will be the cheapest! This one shows separate prices *au comptoir* and *à la salle-terrasse.*
One of the cheapest soft drinks is SIROP fruit flavouring added to *eau minérale* or *limonade.* You could ask for *Vittel/citron, Perrier/cassis, Évian/fraise.*

BOISSONS PILOTE		Comptoir	Salle Terrasse
CATEGORIE ( )			
CAFE	la tasse	1.00	1.50
EAU MINERALE	le petit verre	0.75	1.25
NON GAZEUSE	le grand verre	1.20	1.70
— 1/4 flacon ou ration unitaire		—	—
LIMONADE	le petit verre	0.90	1.40
	le grand verre	1.50	2.00
— 1/4 flacon ou ration unitaire		—	—
BOISSON AUX FRUITS	pt. verre	1.00	1.50
OU AU JUS DE FRUITS	gd. verre	1.75	2.25
— 1/4 flacon ou ration unitaire		—	—
LAIT	le petit verre	1.00	1.50
—	le grand verre	1.80	2.30
BIERE	le 1/2 pression	3.00	3.60
—	bouteille	3.80	4.30
ADJUVANT SIROP	au pt. verre	0.10	0.30
AJOUTE A UNE	gd verre flacon	0.30	0.40
BOISSON PILOTE	SERVICE		
15% en Sus			

If you are going to have your drink sitting down, then wait for the waiter to come to you – don't go to the bar first. There's no need to leave a tip, unless you see a sign saying *service non compris,* in which case leave about 15% of the bill. If you're not sure, ask the waiter, *Le service est compris?*

The BOISSONS PILOTE notice shows set prices of various popular drinks. Brand names are not shown and the drinks shown are the cheapest drinks in the café. It shows the size of cup or glass used and even gives quantities, right down to the number of *centilitres* the cup or glass will hold.

25cl = ¼ litre = under ½ pint
50cl = ½ litre = under 1 pint

— What would *you* order from this list?

— What do *gd verre* and *pt verre* mean?

— It's cheaper to have drinks *au comptoir.* How much more do you pay to have these drinks on the *terrasse?*

  a small glass of lemonade
  a black coffee
  a small mineral water

— Is service charge included?

— If your bill comes to 4.50F how much service charge will you leave?

— What does *en sus* mean?

Food in the café

** some *cafés* allow you to bring your own food with you. You then order a drink to have with it.

** A *café-restaurant* will serve full such as sandwiches, hard-boiled eggs and *croque-monsieur*.

** A *bar* will only serve drinks.

** a *brasserie* will serve food as well as drinks.

** A *café-restaurant* will serve full meals.

Practise asking for some of these drinks

1 un café
2 un Orangina
3 une bouteille de chocolat froid
4 une tasse de chocolat chaud
5 un Joker
6 un verre de lait
7 un verre de limonade
8 un jus d'orange
9 un Perrier

Sophie's checklist

☐ Practise asking for the drinks and food shown on these pages.

☐ Check prices before you order. Study the **Boissons pilote** carefully. Find the cheapest non-alcoholic drinks.

CoffeeCoffee**Coffee**

Un café au lait
Large white breakfast coffee

Un café-crème
Smaller white coffee served all day

Un express
Very strong small black coffee

Un café
Small black coffee

Let's go shopping (2)

You'll find that many of the things you see in the shops in France will be the same as items on sale in Britain.

St Michael
CRACK' PAIN EXTRA-FIN
(à la farine de seigle complet)
PAS PLUS DE 18 CALORIES PAR TRANCHE
Crack'pain ne peut aider l'amaigrissement qu'en faisant partie d'un régime où la ration de calories est contrôlée.

Un Sachet   2 tasses de thé

Mode d'emploi: Verser l'eau bouillante et remuer immédiatement. Laisser infuser 3 à 4 minutes et remuer de nouveau avant de servir.

IMPORTÉ ET EMBALLÉ EN GRANDE-BRETAGNE POUR LE COMPTE DE: MARKS & SPENCER LTD. BAKER ST., LONDON, ENGLAND

MARKS & SPENCER (FRANCE) S.A. 6-8 RUE DES MATHURINS, 75009, PARIS

S.A. MARKS & SPENCER (BELGIUM) N.V. Bd. E. JACQMAIN 6, R.C.B. 378233 1000 BRUXELLES H.R.B.

These labels are from packets bought in a branch of a big supermarket chain in *Britain*.
— Which shop is it?

— Why is the explanation for making tea so detailed?

— Next time you go to a branch of this shop, read the French on some of the labels. It will nearly always have the English next to it. Are labels printed in two languages for *all* types of goods sold in the shop? Why?

— Look in the food department of the shop. Find out what Crack' Pain is. Does it sound more appetising in French or in English? Compare other food names.
— Find one other large chain store in Britain

which labels goods in more than one language.

Self-Service Libre-Service Self-Service Libre-Service

Most small grocery shops are now *self-service*. They may be called simply

| Alimentation | or | Comestibles | or | Épicerie |

Supermarket chains to look out for are:

| Codex | Prisunic | Monoprix |

EUROMARCHÉ

A *hypermarché* is the name for a big supermarket selling virtually all types of goods. These include

Mammouth

Euromarché

Carrefour

mammouth

KORRIGANS
CENTRE COMMERCIAL
RALLYE
HYPERMARCHÉS BREST - QUIMPER - MORLAIX - LANNION

A *centre commercial* is a collection of different shops in one big shopping centre. These are always on the outskirts of towns. You really need a car to get to one. Parking is free and you take your trolley around all the different shops with you. You'll see big signs on buildings advertising centres commerciaux, telling you how far away from one you are.

RALLYE à 10 Km
SUR LA ROUTE DE QUIMPER

Names to look out for:

| Continent | Rallye | Korrigans |

Compare their prices!

CENTRE COMMERCIAL
KORRIGANS
Lanriec-Concarneau RN : 783

SUPER-MARCHÉ

CONTINENT

HOMME

Tee-shirt imprimé - ras de cou - manches courtes - 100 % coton - tailles page - homme - 1/2 patron - patron - colors · 3 dessins assortis	F 17,55
Pantalon toile coton - 100 % coton 2 poches italiennes - 1 poche à rabat dos - tailles 38 à 48 - colors assortis	F 59,50
Blouson 100 % nylon - manches raglan col officier - 2 poches - fermeture à glissière bas - tailles 5 - 6 - 7 - 8 - 9 - colors assortis	F 47,82
Maillot de bain imprimé - 83 % polyamide - 17 % lycra - forme boxer - tailles 2 - 3 - 4 - 5 - colors assortis	F 13,50
Chemisette écossaise - 65 % polyester - 35 % coton - manches courtes - tailles 36 à 44 colors · 3 écossais assortis	F 34,28

Where and when?

Don't shop at lunch-time – 12-2pm (outside Paris). Shops you may find open at lunch-time will be *boulangeries, hypermarchés* and *centres commerciaux.*

Don't shop or change money on MONDAYS. Banks are usually shut, and it's a day off for most shopkeepers too.

Do expect to find some shops open on SUNDAY mornings – always *boulangeries/pâtisseries* usually *charcuteries, alimentation, self-service.* The *pâtisseries,* in particular, are popular on Sundays – it's common to have lovely fresh *pâtisseries* for dessert after a family Sunday lunch.

Do shop at the market for cheese, sweets, clothes, pottery, as well as fruit and vegetables.

Do look out for sales and end of line bargains.

Sophie's Checklist

Check your sizes!

** Would you buy a T-shirt that was
grand ☐   moyen ☐   petit ☐

** Work out your French shoe size. Take your British shoe size and add it to the number 33.
If you take a size 4 shoe:
$$33 + 4 = 37$$
Your French shoe size will be
Trente-sept

** Measure yourself with a centimetre tape. Write down the following measurements:
waist ☐   hips ☐   chest ☐
inside leg ☐   neck ☐

** Remember to take with you things which can be more expensive in France, such as items from a chemist's shop – tissues, sun-tan cream, medicines, films for your camera.

Which Go Together?

- C'est trop grand !
- C'est trop petit !
- C'est trop étroit !
- C'est trop large !
- C'est trop long !
- C'est trop court !
- C'est trop cher !

Extra Extra

*** Note down the names of any French products on sale in Britain. Look in your local supermarket, chemist's shop, market and off-licence. When you get to France, find the same products in French shops, and compare prices.

*** What do the letters EEC stand for? Give another name for the EEC. Do some research and ask around! Do people think that Britain's entry into the EEC has had any effect on food prices.

Keeping in touch

You can buy stamps...

– in post offices (**bureaux de poste**). Look for the counter marked **Affranchissements** or **Timbres-Poste**. Buy your stamps singly, or in carnets or books.

– in all tobacconist shops (**bureaux de tabac**). The red carrot-shaped sign tells you where the tabac is. Tobacco used to be sold in bundles shaped like carrots – hence the sign and its name.

– from stamp machines (**Distributeurs automatiques**). They are yellow.

Look at the postal rates.
How much is it to send a post card to Britain?
How would you ask for stamps for two postcards to Britain?

CARTES POSTALES	Ordinaires ou illustrées avec correspondance
Tarif général	
Allemagne (Rép. féd.) Belgique, Canada, Danemark Grande-Bretagne, Irlande, Italie, Liechtenstein, Luxembourg, Pays-Bas, Suisse et Saint-Marin	1,20

Sophie's checklist

– Write out your address and phone number in France. Give a copy to your parents. Write out the full postal and telephone codes. Your address in France has a 5 figure postal code.

– Take a list of addresses of friends and family you may want to send post cards to.

– Practise asking for stamps for post cards.

– What else does a postman deliver besides letters and parcels?

Vocabulary	Lexique
Post Office	Bureau de poste
Open	Ouvert
Closed	Fermé
Air mail counter	Guichet de la poste aérienne
Poste restante counter (general delivery counter)	Guichet de la poste restante
Sender	Expéditeur
Addressee	Destinataire
Postage stamp	Timbre-poste
Postage stamps for collection	Timbres-poste pour collection
Letter box	Boîte aux lettres
Address	Adresse
Change of address	Modification d'adresse
Air mail	Par avion
Packet	Paquet
Printed matter	Imprimé
Newspaper	Journal

> You may need to contact someone quickly when you can't reach them by telephone.

You can send a telegram from a post office or by telephone. There is a minimum charge for 10 words inside France and 7 words outside France. Use 7 words to tell your family you will be arriving home on a different day and at a different time.

TÉLÉGRAMME N° 698

(telegram form)

Telephones

You need change for the phone.
5F 1F ½F 20c

You can telephone from:
– a **cabine téléphonique.**

There are 85,000 in France! You'll find them in the street, and at bus stops.
– a **post office.** There are 18,000 post offices in France.
– a **café or your hotel.** It will probably cost more to telephone from either of these places.

SPECIAL CALLS

Personal calls (**Avec préavis personnel**)
Charges start only when the person you want to speak to has been contacted.

Reverse charge calls (**En PCV**)
These calls are paid for by the person you are calling.

Area telephone codes

Avec indication de durée et de prix
The operator lets you know the time and price of the call after you've finished.
For any of these special services call
Renseignements – Information

Réclamations – Complaints
Télégraphe – Telegrams
Police-secours – Police and Emergency
Pompiers – Fire

Work and play

I work in an office of the S.N.C.F. — the French railways.

People usually work to earn money to buy necessities such as food and to spend the remainder doing things they want to do.

So they live where they can get work.

The photographs show some of the places where people work in France and some of the jobs they do.

And I work in the bureau de poste.

1 Name the jobs shown in the photos.
2 Which of these jobs are you most likely to find in a city, in a village?
3 What are the main occupations of the people living in your town in Britain?
4 What type of industries do you find near your home?
5 Do they only provide work for the people living near your home or do they attract people from elsewhere?

What do most people in France do for a living?

About a hundred years ago most people worked on the land. The great majority of the population in France was employed in farming or in crafts connected with agriculture. Today the situation has been reversed. Only a small proportion (less than 5%) are occupied in farming. Just over one third of the population are producing goods in manufacturing industries.

And the vast majority provide services to see that the goods reach their destinations. The service sector includes the office workers who prepare the bills, the lorry and train drivers who transport the goods, the people who pack the goods, and so on. It also includes professional people such as teachers and solicitors.

Leisure time

A hundred years ago people worked long hours nearly every day of the year. They only had a break on 'holy days'. Today leisure is taken for granted as an essential ingredient of life.
Leisure time has increased and people take two or more holidays each year. Increased affluence enables them to travel further and further from their homes. Tourism is now big business and makes a significant contribution to the income of most countries. Despite these trends, watching television is the most common leisure activity!

1 What factors do people take into account when planning their holidays?
2 Why do people go on holiday?
3 Make a list of all the jobs that have been created as a result of the growth of tourism?
4 What facilities have been provided in your home town or area for tourists? What sort of things have become tourist attractions?

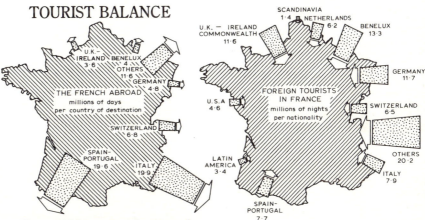

TOURIST BALANCE

THE FRENCH ABROAD
millions of days
per country of destination

U.K.-IRELAND 3·6
BENELUX 4·1
OTHERS 11·6
GERMANY 4·8
SWITZERLAND 6·8
SPAIN-PORTUGAL 19·6
ITALY 19·9

FOREIGN TOURISTS IN FRANCE
millions of nights
per nationality

SCANDINAVIA 1·4
NETHERLANDS 6·2
BENELUX 13·3
U.K. — IRELAND COMMONWEALTH 11·6
GERMANY 11·7
SWITZERLAND 6·5
OTHERS 20·2
ITALY 7·9
U.S.A 4·6
LATIN AMERICA 3·4
SPAIN-PORTUGAL 7·7

1 From which country do most of France's foreign tourists come?
2 To which country do the greatest number of French tourists go?
3 From which country do most of the foreign tourists in your home area come?

Countries receive income from tourists spending money in the country. They then lose the money which their own people spend as tourists in other countries. The diagram shows this 'budget account'.

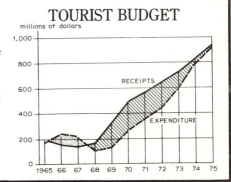

TOURIST BUDGET
millions of dollars

RECEIPTS

EXPENDITURE

1,000
800
600
400
200
0

1965 66 67 68 69 70 71 72 73 74 75

Enjoy yourself !

> Did you know that the first ever moving picture was made by a Frenchman?

Louis and Auguste Lumière

Cinema

Louis Lumière with his brother, Auguste, invented *the cinématographe* – a small rectangular box which could take a film, develop, process, print, wash, dry *and* project it. That was in 1895. The very first moving picture showed workers coming out of the Lumière factory.

Since then, the quality of the French cinema has always been very high. Famous French film directors include: *Jean Renoir, François Truffaut, Agnès Varda, Alain Resnais, Jean-Luc Godard, Louis Malle, Jacques Tati, Jean Vigo.*

N.B.

* The usherette (*l'ouvreuse*) expects a tip for showing you to your seat.

* *Séance permanente* – continuous programme

* V.O. means *version originale*. Subtitles are used.

* V.F. means *version française*. The film has been dubbed.

Sophie's checklist

Find out . . .

What sort of French films are shown here in cinemas? ☐
on television? ☐
Are French films shown on the big circuits, like Odeon and Gaumont? If not, where are they shown? ☐
Are many *comic* French films shown here? ☐
Compare types of American and French films shown on television here. ☐
Try watching a French film on television without looking at the subtitles . ☐
Listen to French radio before you go . ☐
You can get all these on long wave. Try it!
RTL   Europe No 1   France Inter
236KHz   182KHz   164KHz ☐
Use your library. Find the names of the most famous films by these directors, Jean Renoir; Jean-Luc Godard; Agnès Varda; François Truffaut ☐

Days Off

Compare French holidays to yours.

Le premier janvier
On New Year's Day small presents are given to the postman, the dustman and the concierge.

Pâques
Sunday and Monday of Easter are holidays. In the south a special *omelette flambée* is eaten. Chocolate and sugar eggs are given to children.

Le premier mai
La Fête du Travail. There are marches and displays

Sport

Le Football

Association football is played all over France. The *championnat de France,* organised by the Fédération Française de Football (like the F.A.) is played between first division teams. The final is played in the *Parc des Princes* in Paris.

Le Parc des Princes

SPORTS   *Mercredi 10 septembre 1986 • DH – DIX NEUF*

France Soir

Quatre clubs (St-Etienne, Lyon, Bordeaux, Nantes) en tête du championnat de France.

Les Verts s'en sortent bien

Le classement

	Pts	J	G	N	P	bp	bc	Diff.
1 ST-ETIENNE	13	9	6	1	2	21	10	+11
2 BORDEAUX	13	9	5	3	1	15	5	+10
3 LYON	13	9	5	3	1	17	10	+7
4 NANTES	13	9	6	1	2	18	12	+6
5 PARIS S.-G.	12	9	4	4	1	13	13	0
6 MONACO	11	9	4	3	2	18	9	+9
7 TOURS	11	9	4	3	2	19	16	+3
8 LENS	9	9	3	3	3	14	14	0
9 NICE	9	9	3	3	3	11	11	0

FOOTBALL

Un derby rhodanien sans vainqueur (1-1)

Lyon et Saint-Étienne toujours côte à côte

Le Rugby

Rugby Union is very popular, particularly in the south and south west. International matches are played on Saturdays, national games on Sundays. The *Tournoi des Cinq Nations* is played between France, England, Wales, Ireland and... which is the fifth?

15.05
En direct du stade de
Murrayfield à Edimbourg
Rugby
**TOURNOI DES
CINQ NATIONS**
FR3
ÉCOSSE-FRANCE

Le Cyclisme

Possibly the most popular sport. Amateur cyclists of all ages can be seen training on Sunday mornings on major and minor roads throughout France. Races are organised right through the year – the most famous being the *Tour de France.*

Bernard Hinault is one of the most successful of France's cyclists.

organised by trades unions. Give a buttonhole of lily of the valley to friends.

L'Ascension
The 6th Thursday after Easter. Many people take a spring holiday during L'Ascension and...

Pentecôte
The 7th Sunday and Monday after Easter.

Le quatorze juillet
La Fête Nationale celebrates the taking of the Bastille prison, marking the beginning of the big revolution. All over France houses are decorated with flags.

In the evening there are often fireworks and dances in the streets. In Paris there's a big military procession on the Champs-Elysées.

Le quinze août
L'Assomption. Biggest fête of the summer. In many towns there are religious processions and folklore festivals.

Le premier novembre
La Toussaint — La Fête du

Souvenir – flowers, especially chrysanthemum are laid on relatives' graves.

Le onze novembre
The Armistice, marking the end of the war in 1918. The President lays a wreath on the tomb of the unknown soldier in Paris. The dead of two world wars are remembered.

Le vingt-cinq décembre
Noël – Midnight Mass on Christmas Eve, followed by traditional bell ringing (*le réveillon*). Children put shoes by the fire. *Père Noël* (Saint Nicolas) will put presents in them during the night.

There are about 130 competitors, who sweep through towns and villages over a 20 day period. They are followed by huge cavalcades of cars, vans containing spares, and television and film crews. The leaders of the race can be picked out by the colour of the jerseys they wear, green for the winner of the previous day's stage, yellow for the overall leader (*le maillot jaune*).

On the road

These are your **ON THE SPOT** pages. They have dark edges so that you can find them easily. **IN FRANCE** set aside a little time each day to look at the **ON THE SPOT** activities.

Spot the signs

As you see these *types* of road signs, tick them off.

Find out ...

1 why the names of towns are sometimes crossed out.
2 the difference between roads marked A, N and D.
3 how much petrol costs per litre. How many litres could you get for 50 francs? Is it more expensive than it is in Britain?
4 the names of the 2 *grades* of petrol. Find the names of as many *brands* of petrol as you can.
5 on what sort of vehicle you would see the letters TIR.
6 the differences between French and British traffic lights.
7 the French for toll. You pay a toll on most French motorways.
8 the names of two sets of twinned towns you pass through.
9 the French for town centre.
10 what the ⑨⓪ sign refers to. It must be shown on the back of a car for one year after the driver has passed the driving test, or also if the car has snow tyres on.

How to Change Kilometres to Miles		
80 kilometres = ??? miles		
a Halve the number of kilometres		= **40**
b Work out 1 quarter of that number		= **10**
c Add the two together	40 + 10 =	**50** miles
So 80 kilometres is **50** miles		

Crops

As you travel through the countryside, try to recognise some of the crops we grow.

Because France extends over 1,100 kilometres from north to south, and over 900 kilometres from west to east, it is possible to grow a wide variety of crops. These photos show just a few of the leading crops.

— Which crops did you see on your journey?

— Which are grown mainly in the north of France and which mainly in the south?
— What are the most important crops grown in your area in France? Who decides to grow these crops and what factors influence the decision?

Sunflowers in the Périgord

Maize and wheat

Vineyards in the Lot valley

Tobacco plants in the Lot valley

Where are they from?

The last two numbers on a car's registration plate tell you which area the car is from. The areas are called *départements* and are shown on this map.
What's the name of the département you're staying in?
On your journey make a note of car registration numbers.

- Find out which départements they are from.
- How many can you spot which are *not* from the area you are travelling through?

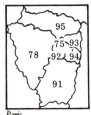

Paris

If you are passing through Seine-Maritime most of the cars you see will have numbers ending in — 76 . But during July and August most French people go away on holiday and many travel to the seaside. So in those months you may see a lot of cars which are not from the local area.

This car is from the Pas-de-Calais *area.* — 62

01	Ain
02	Aisne
03	Allier
04	Alpes (Basses)
05	Alpes (Hautes)
06	Alpes-Maritimes
07	Ardèche
08	Ardennes
09	Ariège
10	Aube
11	Aude
12	Aveyron
13	Bouches-du-Rhône
14	Calvados
15	Cantal
16	Charente
17	Charente-Maritime
18	Cher
19	Corrèze
20	Corse
21	Côte d'Or
22	Côtes-du-Nord
23	Creuse
24	Dordogne
25	Doubs
26	Drôme
27	Eure
28	Eure-et-Loir
29N	Nord-Finistère
29S	Sud-Finistère
30	Gard
31	Garonne (Haute)
32	Gers
33	Gironde
34	Hérault
35	Ille-et-Vilaine
36	Indre
37	Indre-et-Loire
38	Isère
39	Jura
40	Landes
41	Loir-et-Cher
42	Loire
43	Loire (Haute)
44	Loire-Atlantique
45	Loiret
46	Lot
47	Lot-et-Garonne
48	Lozère
49	Maine-et-Loire
50	Manche
51	Marne
52	Marne (Haute)
53	Mayenne
54	Meurthe-et-Moselle
55	Meuse
56	Morbihan
57	Moselle
58	Nièvre
59	Nord
60	Oise
61	Orne
62	Pas-de-Calais
63	Puy-de-Dôme
64	Pyrénées (Basses)
65	Pyrénées (Hautes)
66	Pyrénées Orient
67	Rhin (Bas)
68	Rhin (Haut)
69	Rhône
70	Saône (Haute)
71	Saône-et-Loire
72	Sarthe
73	Savoie
74	Savoie (Haute)
75	Paris (Ville de)
76	Seine-Maritime
77	Seine-et-Marne
78	Yvelines
79	Sèvres (Deux)
80	Somme
81	Tarn
82	Tarn-et-Garonne
83	Var
84	Vaucluse
85	Vendée
86	Vienne
87	Vienne (Haute)
88	Vosges
89	Yonne
90	Belfort (Ter.)
91	Essonne
92	Hauts de Seine
93	Seine St-Denis
94	Val de Marne
95	Val d'Oise

Look out for foreign cars and lorries. Fit these international registration letters with the countries they represent.

Belgium   Germany   Italy   France   Switzerland   Austria   Holland

NL   F   B   D   I   A   CH   E   GB   P   Fl   L   DK   S

Denmark   Liechtenstein   Portugal   Great Britain   Sweden   Spain   Luxembourg

Speak up!

39

Settling in

Speak up !

Write the correct words in the speech balloons.

Look around...

the place you're staying in.
See if you can find these things.
TICK them off as you find them.

— A notice informing you of what
  to do in case of fire ☐
— A notice in the lift indicating
  maximum load ☐
— Shutters on the outside
  of the windows ☐
— A notice behind the bedroom
  door giving room prices ☐

— A coffee making
  machine ☐
— A notice saying
  ouvert/fermé ☐
— A notice saying
  COMPLET or CHAMBRES ☐
— La caisse ☐
— Le restaurant ☐
— Le bar ☐
— La salle de bains ☐
— An ashtray with the
  name of a drink on it ☐
— A menu ☐

Un Couvert

1	un verre	2	un couteau
3	une fourchette	4	une tasse
5	une soucoupe	6	une cuiller
7	une assiette	8	du sel
9	du poivre	10	du pain

Which is which? Write the correct
numbers in the boxes.

Practise saying that items are
missing and that you would like them.

Example: Je n'ai pas de couteau. Je
voudrais un couteau, s'il vous plaît.

Je ne peux pas ouvrir la porte de
ma chambre.

Est-ce qu'elle a dit que c'est au
quatrième étage?

Pardon, madame. Il n' y a pas de
serviettes dans ma chambre.

Problems Problems Problems

French hotels are pretty good, but be prepared to deal with problems.

What will you say if...

1 you want to know which floor your room is on?
2 you've forgotten your room number?
3 you want tea, milk, bread, butter and jam for breakfast?
4 the window is jammed?
5 you can't lock your door?
6 the light bulb is broken?
7 you want your door key?
8 there is no plug in the wash basin?
9 you want to leave your money and valuables in the hotel safe?

Choose from these sentences

La fenêtre s'est coincée

L'ampoule est cassée

Il n'y a pas de bonde dans le lavabo.

Puis-je avoir la clef de ma chambre, s'il vous plaît?

Je voudrais un thé complet, s'il vous plaît.

Quel est le numéro de ma chambre? Je m'appelle.......

Je voudrais consigner de l'argent à l'hôtel, s'il vous plaît.

Ma chambre est à quel étage, s'il vous plaît?

Je ne peux pas fermer la porte de ma chambre.

Extra Extra

**** Look around your hotel. Are there any signs which tell you what you can and can't do? Make a list of them and write down whether you think the requests are reasonable or not, and why.
**** Notice what the people who work at the hotel do. Make a list of the jobs which must be done daily. Does one person do more than one job?
**** Ask for a brochure or card advertising the hotel.

Above: *L'Hôtel Negresco, Nice*

Speak up !

41

Bon Appétit

In the Street

Which snacks can you buy from this van?

You'll have lots of opportunities to buy snack foods in the street. But be careful, they may be expensive and it might be better to wait for your evening meal at the hotel.

What else can you buy here besides *crêpes*? What do we call *crêpes*? You can get them made from white flour (*froment*) or buckwheat flour (*blé noir*), and sweet or savoury.

Many people feel that crêpes are a bit of a 'rip-off'. Have a look at prices. Do you agree?

As you see these *makes* of ice-cream advertised around the streets, tick them off. Can you add any others? How many *flavours* of ice-cream can you find? In a note book, make a list. Write the meanings by the side as you try them!

J'aime la barbe à papa!

Speak up!

Asking for ice-cream

Extra Extra

** Go to a *pâtisserie*. As you find the following things, tick them off:

un éclair   un moka
un chou à la crème
un baba au rhum
une religieuse
une mille-feuille
une tarte aux fruits

** Find out whether the region you are in has a

Extra Extra

spécialité de cuisine.

** Find out from the Syndicat or the hotel whether any cheeses are made in the area. If there are, buy a little (*cinquante grammes*) to taste. Do the same for local *charcuterie*.

** Find out whether there are any vineyards in

Speak up!

Mini-Menu Translator

Here are some of the terms you'll come across. Don't expect to find everything here!

agneau	lamb
andouille	type of sausage
assiette anglaise	plate of cooked meats
barbe à papa	candy floss
bigorneaux	winkles
betteraves	beetroot
bifteck	steak

Extra Extra

the area. Are you near any of the *main* wine producing areas? Find out from this map.

bien cuit	well cooked
bleu	of steak – barely cooked
boeuf	beef
boule	scoop of ice cream
carottes râpées	grated carrot
champignons	mushrooms
charcuterie	cooked meat
chou	cabbage or type of cake
chou-fleur	cauli-flower
coquillages	shell-fish
coquille	scallop
côte	chop (of meat)
crabe	crab
crêpe	pancake
crevettes	shrimps
croque-monsieur	cheese and ham grilled in sandwich
crudités	raw vegetables in dressing
crustacés	crabs, lobsters, oysters etc
cuisses de grenouille	frogs' legs
dégustation	tasting
écrevisses	prawns

épinards	spinach
escalope	thin slice of veal or pork
escargots	snails
farci	stuffed
faux-filet	type of steak
frites	chips
friture	small fried fish
gigot d'agneau	leg of lamb
hareng	herring
haricots verts	French beans
haricots secs	dried beans
huîtres	oysters
jambon	ham
langoustines	Dublin bay prawns
lapin	rabbit
légumes	vegetables
lièvre	hare
maquereaux	mackerel
marrons	chestnuts
merlan	whiting
moules	mussels
niçoise	(salad) with tuna and olives
nouilles	noodles
oeufs	eggs
petits gris	type of snails
petits pois	peas
pintade	guinea-fowl

pommes (de terre)	potatoes
frites	chips
purée de	mashed
vapeur	steamed
poisson	fish
porc	pork
potage	soup
poulet	chicken
quiche	open tart
radis	radishes
rillettes	chopped cooked pork
riz	rice
rognons	kidneys
rôti	roast
salade	lettuce with French dressing
saucisse	sausage to cook
saucisson	sausage, no need to cook
saumon	salmon
sup = supplément	pay extra
terrine	potted meat
thon	tuna fish
veau	veal
viande	meat
vinaigrette	oil and vinegar salad dressing
volaille	poultry
yaourt	yoghurt

Around the town

As you're sightseeing, have a look at some street names.

Place du 8 Novembre 1944

BOULEVARD DE LA POSTE

RUE LOUIS LUMIÈRE

Streets are often named after *places*

politicians or war heroes
writers and scientists
important dates

RUE DU GÉNÉRAL DE GAULLE

Rue du Maréchal-Foch

PLACE D'ANGLETERRE

** Find street names which fit into each of the categories on the left.

** Find an example of
un Boulevard
une Rue
une Avenue
une Place
un Quai
une Allée
une Promenade

Who's who?

Write the correct numbers in the boxes. if you're not sure, then SPEAK UP! and ask someone in the street.

1 *une femme-agent*
2 *un gendarme*
3 *un agent de police*
4 *un pompier*
5 *un facteur*

Pardon, monsieur l'agent...
Je suis gendarme.

Pardon, monsieur l'agent...
Je suis facteur.

Pardon, monsieur l'agent... où est la gendarmerie?
Oh, là là!

By the Way...
The *facteur* delivers newspapers as well as letters.
Firemen are often volunteers, doing other jobs most of the time. The office of the *agent* is the *commissariat de police*. The *agent* is the ordinary policeman in a large town – over 10,000 inhabitants. Policemen and women usually carry revolvers.

Les amis du peuple! Don't argue with a *gendarme!* Gendarmes police towns of less than 10,000 people. Their office is the *Gendarmerie Nationale*. They are also reponsible for road policing in the *département*. They can fine motorists on the spot for traffic offences. They are armed and can use revolvers in self-defence. They are really part of the army and can act as military police.

What's Missing?

There's something missing from each of these pictures.
Look around the town and find out what's been left out.

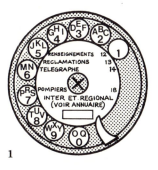

1

2

3

4

5

6

Speak up!

What would you say if...

1 you stepped on someone's foot in the street?
   a. Salut, monsieur! ☐
   b. Pardon, monsieur! ☐
   c. De rien, monsieur! ☐

2 you wanted to find the nearest metro station?
   a. Pour aller à la gare, s'il vous plaît? ☐
   b. Pour aller à la station, s'il vous plaît? ☐
   c. Y a-t-il une station de metro près d'ici? ☐

3 you wanted to know what time the tourist office opened?
   a. Le Syndicat d'Initiative est ouvert à quelle heure? ☐
   b. Le Syndicat d'Initiative est fermé. ☐
   c. Quelle heure est-il? ☐

Extra Extra

Look around and find...

1 the busiest street. Why is it so?
2 the most popular café. Why is it so?
3 the largest shop.
4 the highest building. Go to the top. Look at the view.
5 buildings flying the French flag.
6 the quietest place.
7 the most expensive hotel.
8 the most interesting area.
9 the oldest houses.
10 Look back at Sophie's Checklist on *page 19* and compare the items on her list.

Signs and adverts

A

See if you can find any French graffiti.
What would **À bas l'école** mean?
Write down any other slogans you see and try to work out what they mean. Ask for help if necessary!

B

Find as many adverts for British goods as you can.
Look for cars, toothpaste, food, washing powders...

C

When you're in a supermarket ... listen!

Listen to the loudspeaker voice.

1 How do you know that the voice is about to start?
2 Why is it there?
3 What is it advertising?
4 Can you see any visual adverts for the same products?
5 Is there any evidence that this form of advertising works? Look in people's baskets and find out.

D Where would you find the following signs?
See how many you can find.
When you see them, tick them off.

ENTRÉE	SORTIE	POUSSEZ	TIREZ
LIBRE	OCCUPÉ	CAISSE	MESSIEURS
DAMES	HOMMES	FEMMES	GENDARMERIE
GUICHET	CHIEN MÉCHANT	EAU POTABLE	
COMPLET	PROPRIÉTÉ PRIVÉE	SOLDES	

INTERDIT AUX MOINS DE DIX-HUIT ANS

Which Go Together?

Link the objects on the left with places they belong to

PLACEZ CE TICKET DERRIERE VOTRE PARE-BRISE
VISIBLE DE L'EXTERIEUR

EXPIRATION DU TEMPS
DE STATIONNEMENT   7349127

SEMAINE JOUR	HEURE MINUTE	SOMME PAYÉE
24 Lu	14 47	01 00
24 Lu	14 47	01 00

SEMAINE JOUR   HEURE MINUTE   SOMME PAYÉE
AIDE A MEMOIRE   7349127

> It's my first time in Paris and I can't find my way in the metro. I want to go to OPÉRA and I'm stuck at ODÉON. Can you help me?

Luckily Sophie has been to Paris before and can help Gérard out!

Follow the signs showing

DIRECTION Porte de Clignancourt

Get out at **CHÂTELET**

At **Châtelet** look for the signs saying

CORRESPONDANCES – this means **Change**

Take the

DIRECTION Fort D'Aubervilliers to OPÉRA

N.B. If you can manage to pronounce *all* the names on the Paris metro map. then your reading of French must be *excellent!* Which do you think is the *most* difficult?

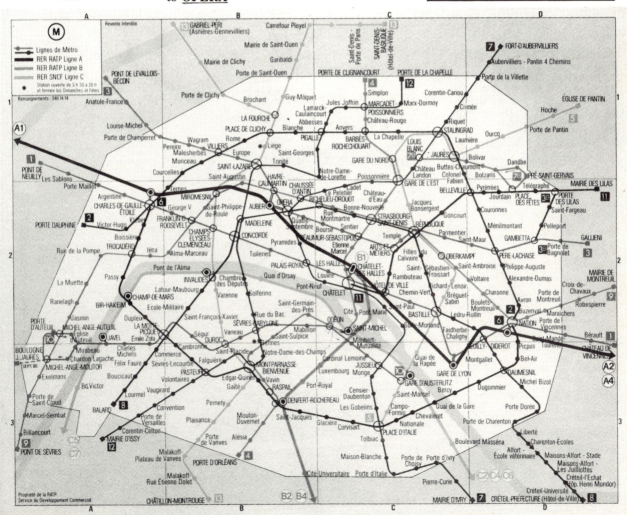

Let's go shopping

When you're choosing presents to take home, **do** choose things which are typically French! Compare prices! Ask yourself whether you can buy the same or similar things at home. Remember that records, clothes and sweets are probably cheaper at home.

Your parents may like a 'taste of France.'

Some things will cost you nothing, but will certainly remind you of France.
Souvenir in French means 'to remember'.

Shells from the beach
Brochures from the hotel
Unused, wrapped sugar lumps from the café
Tickets from museums, buses, metro, or cinemas

Fairly cheap souvenirs

Postcards,	Set of plastic boules
Newspapers,	Stamps
Magazines	Models

Have a look at different types of tinned delicacies

Marrons (chestnuts)   *Coquilles au whisky*
Escargots (snails)   *Sardines aux truffes*
Cuisses de grenouille (frogs' legs)
Maquereaux au vin blanc
Thon à l'Indienne

**** At the supermarket find out...
How many types of tinned tuna fish you can buy in France? See who can find the highest number. Write the names and varieties down in your note book.

How much to ask for?

Cent cinquante grammes de pâté

Une bouteille de champagne!

Une boîte d'escargots

Deux cents grammes de fromage

Deux tranches de jambon

Cent grammes de bonbons (dragées)

Une livre de pêches

Un pot de moutarde

Une boîte de marrons

Un paquet de biscuits

Weights

100 grammes = just under 4oz
400 grammes = just under 1lb
Une livre = un demi-kilo = just over 1lb
Un kilo = 1,000 grammes = about 2¼lb

Volume

1 litre = 10 decilitres (dl) = 1¾ pints
Un demi-litre = just over ¾ pint
Un quart = just under ½ pint
1 decilitre (dl) = 6 tablespoons
1 centilitre = 1 dessertspoon
5 millilitres = standard medicine spoon size
4.54 litres = 1 gallon = 8 pints

Extra Extra Extra Extra Extra Extra

The photos show different types of shops you'll see **On the spot.** When you're shopping take a note book with you. When you spot each of these shops, write down what each one sells or does. Write down the names of any other types of shops you come across. What do they sell?

Look for a *PRESSING* **On the spot.**
Find out the prices for cleaning:
une veste   une jupe
un pantalon
Write down the names of as many fabrics as you can – in French.
Find out how many ways there are to indicate that prices are lowered. For example: LIQUIDATION

RABAIS   SOLDES

Speak up!

Je voudrais changer dix livres
Votre passeport?

Je voudrais de la monnaie d'une pièce de 10 francs.

Vous avez des journaux anglais?
Je n'en ai pas!

At the shoe shop

Je voudrais des chaussures comme ça!
Comme ça? Quelle pointure?
Trente-sept!
Formidable, mademoiselle! Cent soixante-dix francs!
Oh! Mes pauvres pieds! Trop haut! Trop étroit! Trop petit! Et trop cher!

At the market

When you're in the market, find out...

* how many *jours de marché* there are each week.

* what the *Place du Marché* is used for when there is no market there.

* what the cheese stall sells, apart from cheese.

* which vegetables and fruit are locally grown.

* which fruits have to be imported into France.

* which are the cheapest fruits. Why are they the cheapest?

49

At the café

I don't only go to cafés for a drink. In fact I often go to a café after school, stay all evening and have only one drink. I go there to meet friends, chat and play some of the games you'll find in cafés IN FRANCE.

Which are which?

1 un flipper

2 un juke-box

3 un croque-monsieur

4 une bière

What would you say if...

1 you wanted a cheese sandwich?
- a. Garçon, du fromage, s'il vous plaît! ☐
- b. Un croque-monsieur, s'il vous plaît! ☐
- c. Un sandwich au fromage, s'il vous plaît! ☐

2 you wanted the waiter to bring you the bill?
- a. L'addition, s'il vous plaît. ☐
- b. Service, s'il vous plaît. ☐
- c. L'argent, s'il vous plaît. ☐

3 you wanted to find the lavatory?
- a. Où est la sortie, s'il vous plaît? ☐
- b. Où sont les toilettes, s'il vous plaît? ☐
- c. Le lavabo, s'il vous plaît? ☐

4 you didn't know whether to leave a tip or not?
- a. Le service est compris? ☐
- b. L'addition, s'il vous plaît? ☐
- c. C'est combien? ☐

5 you wanted a hot chocolate and the waiter has brought you a tea?
- a. Un thé? Mais je voudrais un chocolat chaud. ☐
- b. Un chocolat chaud? Mais je voudrais un thé. ☐
- c. Oh! Merci, monsieur! ☐

6 you wanted change for the juke-box?
- a. Pouvez-vous me donner le juke-box, s'il vous plaît? ☐
- b. Avez-vous des pièces de un franc, s'il vous plaît? Voici une pièce de cinq francs. ☐
- c. Je voudrais changer de l'argent. ☐

7 the juke-box didn't work?
- a. Le flipper ne marche pas. ☐
- b. Zut! ☐
- c. Le juke-box ne marche pas. ☐

Extra Extra Extra Extra Extra Extra

Make a list of the drinks you've tried. Do you feel you've been adventurous enough?

Make a list of the cafés you've been to. Compare the names with names of pubs in Britain.

What is a **café-tabac**?

Apart from normal café drinks and food, list some of the other things sold in a café-tabac.

You may see the letters P.M.U. in some cafés. They stand for **Pari Mutuel Urbain.**
Ask around and find out

what it is for. On which day of the week is the P.M.U. most likely to be important?

When you are in a brasserie find out how many English words, such as *hot-dog,* are included on the menu.

LOOK AND SEE!
Find out as many
of these things as
you can!

Which is the most popular café in the place you're staying in? Why is it so popular?
Is there a café which is more popular with 1) older people 2) younger people? Why?

What is the most popular drink among young French people? Ask its name. Try it.

Normally you pay for drinks when you want to *leave* the café. On what occasions might the waiter ask you to pay for drinks at the same time as he serves them?

Are there any restrictions in cafés concerning age? How are age limits shown? Copy down part of the sign which you'll find in all cafés telling you of age restrictions.

Take a note of opening and closing times of cafés in your town. When do they close?

Find the French for
— a lemon tea
— a hot chocolate
— the bill
— a pâté sandwich

Find the English for
— une infusion
— frites
— non compris
— un oeuf dur

Speak up!

Enjoy yourself...

...as a reporter on the spot!

Find

— The French word for newspapers and the symbol which goes with it.
— A *Maison des Jeunes*. What is it? What goes on there?
— A game of *boules* in progress. What is the aim of the game? Where is it played? What are the boules made of?
— As many of the newspapers and magazines shown on these pages as you can. As you find them, write the names in your note book and note the prices. How much would Le Figaro cost in Great Britain?

Speak up!

Un Interview

Ask someone if you can do a little interview with them. Choose someone at your hotel or in the street.

Excusez-moi, madame, monsieur or mademoiselle, je suis en vacances avec un groupe scolaire de La Grande Bretagne. Puis-je vous poser quelques questions? C'est pour l'école.
Comment vous appelez-vous?
Quelle est votre adresse?
Vous travaillez? Où?
Quelles sont vos distractions préférées?
Qui est votre chanteur préféré?
Et votre sport préféré?
Quelle est votre boisson préférée?
Et votre plat de cuisine préféré?
Où allez-vous passer les grandes vacances?

Vous aimez regarder la télévision? Quelles sont les émissions que vous préférez?
Now answer the questions yourself!

Look around for posters advertising rock groups and concerts. Make a list of French rock stars.

RICKY LAMANT

LE FIGARO

Le Télégramme

ouest france

France-Soir

Extra Extra Extra Extra Extra Extra

* Buy the local paper and *find*

1 the main local news story of the day
2 the main national news story
3 the main international news story
4 the name of the local football team
5 the weather forecast
6 the television programmes
7 the name of one local cinema
8 the French for 'news'

Keeping in touch
How to telephone from France

1 *Décrocher le combiné*
2 *Introduire les pièces*
3 *Si les pièces n'apparaissent pas, appuyer sur le bouton. Attendre la tonalité. Composer le numéro.*
4 *Préparer les pièces. Les introduire au signal.*

Do you put in the money before or after you dial the number?

What do you do if the coins don't drop and you can't see them?
Before you dial the number what must you listen out for?
Why do you have to get more money ready after you have dialled?

When do you put in any extra coins?
If you were making a short, local call, which coin would you use?
5F   1F   0.20F
If you were dialling Britain which coins would you have ready?

The cheapest times to telephone are the evenings, Sundays and holidays

To phone Britain from France...
Write down the complete number and code before you start.
Code from France = 19 44 + your home town code minus 0.

Useful phone numbers in France

If phoning within Paris miss out the number 1.
Horloge parlante (1) 463 84 00
Informations touristiques (1) 723 61 72
Recherche d'identité téléphonique (1) 266 35 35
Renseignments SNCF (1) 261 50 50
Centre national d'informations sur le tourisme et des loisirs (1) 296 63 63
Météo (1) 705 97 39

Which slot would you use to send your mail home?

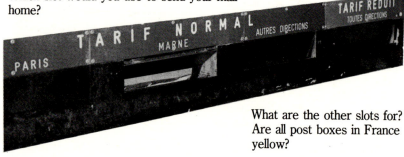

What are the other slots for?
Are all post boxes in France yellow?

Speak up!

Je voudrais des timbres. Allons au bureau de tabac, là-bas!

Combien coûte une carte postale pour La Grande Bretagne?

Un franc dix, madame!

Quatre timbres à un franc dix, s'il vous plaît.

Un...deux...trois... quatre. Voilà, madame.

Ça fait quatre francs quarante, s'il vous plaît.

Voici quatre francs quarante, monsieur.

Merci, madame.

Keeping well!

Speak up!

Say what the problem is!
Fit the correct words with the appropriate pictures.

1 J'ai mal aux dents
2 J'ai mal au bras
3 J'ai mal au ventre
4 J'ai mal au dos
5 J'ai mal à la gorge
6 J'ai mal aux pieds

You get medicines at the *pharmacie*. But be careful! Things are expensive there! The *pharmacien* will offer advice on minor aliments... if not... you'll need *un médecin*.

You pay on the spot for a visit to a doctor in France as well as for a prescription. French people fill in a form and claim most of the money back. You can do this too if you have a form **E111** which you can get from your local office of the Department of Health and Social Security before you leave. In France you take it to the *Caisse Primaire de Sécurité Sociale* at the town hall. To get your form **E111** go to the local DHSS office about a month before you leave and get form **CM1**. Fill it in and you'll be sent your E111!

France – Region by Region

Contents

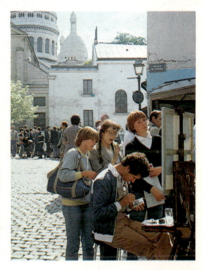

1. *The Gros Horloge, Rouen*
2. *The cliffs at Etretat, Normandy*
3. *A market in La Haye-du-Puits, Normandy*
4. *La Place du Tertre, Paris*
5. *Traditional dress in Brittany*
6. *The Arc de Triomphe, Paris*

Brittany

Like **Astérix**, the cartoon Gallic warrior, the people of Brittany are proud, stubborn and independent. They resisted the Romans so fiercely that it took Caesar himself to defeat them. They managed to maintain their independence from France until 1488.

Like the Welsh, the **Bretons** have their own language which is still understood by about a third of the three million inhabitants.

Above: *Asterix a popular cartoon from France*
Left: *Map showing the movement of Britons into Brittany*

The Pointe du Raz – the Land's End of France

Standing stones

The first traces of civilisation to be found in France are the cave paintings of **Lascaux** in the south west and the **standing stones** of Brittany. About four thousand years ago Brittany was occupied by a sea-faring people who may have come from the Mediterranean.

In **Armorica**, as Brittany was then called, they set up thousands of standing stones, or **megaliths**. Some of them, called **dolmens**, were tombs. They consist of several large rocks, upright in the ground, with a flat rock, like a roof, perched on the top of them. These were probably constructed by piling up a mound of earth, then hauling the flat top up the mound. The earth of the mound was then taken away, leaving a giant stone table. Other standing stones, called **menhirs** (from **men** meaning **stone** and **hir** meaning **long**) have no obvious purpose. But groups of **menhirs,** like those at **Carnac,** were probably temples.

The people of Armorica had close links with the people of western England and Wales. **Stonehenge** is similar to the constructions in Brittany and there are dolmens and menhirs in many parts of Wales. Apart from this very little is known about these people.

The Franklin's Tale

The fourteenth century English writer, **Chaucer**, wrote a story about the black and menacing rocks of Brittany in his **Canterbury Tales**. The **Franklin**, a landowner, tells this story to his fellow pilgrims, on their way to Canterbury.

A landowner from **Finistère**, called **Arveragus**, fell in love with a girl called **Dorigen**. They were happily married and went to live on the coast, overlooking jagged rocks like those of the **Pointe du Raz**. Arveragus went to Britain for two years and while he was away, another local lord, **Aurelius**, fell in love with Dorigen. She was faithful to her husband and, to discourage Aurelius, said jokingly that she would only love him when he had cleared the Brittany coast of rocks. He went to France (then a separate country) and met a magician, who for a large fee agreed to spirit the rocks away. When Dorigen saw what had happened she was frantic. She told her husband, who had since come home. He said that she must keep her word. But when she went to find Aurelius, he realised that he had caused her great misery. So he released her from her promise and Dorigen and Arveragus lived happily ever after.

Land's End

La Pointe du Raz is the western-most point of France. It is in the département of Finistère, meaning land's end. Beyond it is a lighthouse and the **Ile de Sein**. This is a flat, treeless island inhabited by extremely hardy and courageous people. Until the eighteenth century, when they were converted to Christianity, they were almost completely cut off from the mainland. The people of Brittany feared the islanders, because they encouraged shipwrecks and robbed vessels washed up on the dangerous coastline. During the Second World War the islanders showed their independence by refusing to accept the German victory in France. All the men went to England to join General de Gaulle and the Free French. After the war they were all given medals.

The Pardon of Sainte Anne of Auray
Sainte Anne is the patron saint of Brittany. One of the most popular **pardons**, or pilgrimages, in the province takes place at **Auray** every year in early March. The great procession celebrates an event that took place in 1623.

Sainte Anne, the mother of the Virgin Mary, appeared in a vision to a local peasant. She told him that at the very spot he was standing there had been a chapel dedicated to her, almost a thousand years before. Now she wanted a new chapel built. Two years later while digging for the old

building, the peasant found a statue of Sainte Anne. His discovery has been commemorated every year since then.

Many other pardons are held every summer in Brittany. People come from miles around to take part in the procession and the fête afterwards, often wearing traditional costume. Brittany is still the most religious part of France. As a result the people tend to be very conservative, preserving old costumes and customs. Old women can still be seen in black dresses and tall lace hats, sitting in groups making lace by hand or mending fishing nets.

Normandy

Normandy is named after the Normans, the Norsemen who came from Scandinavia. They were great sailors, who raided large parts of Europe. They conquered places as far apart as England and Sicily. In 911 they settled in Normandy. A contemporary writer described the Normans as lavish, greedy, eager for power, enthusiastic huntsmen, fond of fine horses and fine clothing.

Normandy has been the centre of two key moments in the history of France and England.

1 **the invasion of England by William of Normandy in 1066.**

2 **the invasion of France by the allied forces in 1944.**

The tapestry museum and cathedral at Bayeux.

Norman states in the Middle Ages.

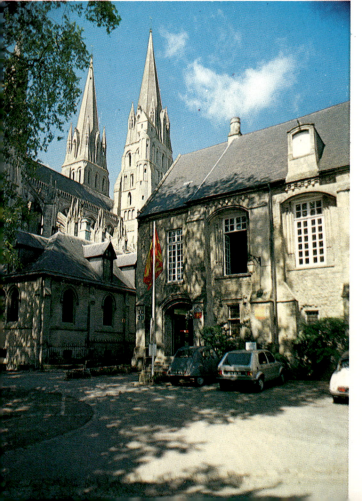

The Norman invasion — William the Conqueror
William Duke of Normandy was adventurous, ambitious and a skilful statesman. His cousin, Edward the Confessor, king of England had promised him his kingdom when he died. An English noble called **Harold** thought otherwise, in spite of the fact that he had given up his claim to the throne when he was William's prisoner a few years earlier.

When Edward died, William planned carefully. He persuaded the Pope to excommunicate Harold. He arranged for the Viking King of Norway to invade northern England and he agreed a truce with his French neighbours, so that Normandy would not be attacked when he was away in England. In September 1066 he assembled an army of 12,000 men in 700 ships. They set out from the tiny port of Barfleur. Harold had only just defeated the Norwegians in the north of England. He hurried south to meet the invasion. On October 14th 1066 the armies met near **Hastings.** The Norman cavalry overwhelmed the English footsoldiers and Harold was killed. William of Normandy became King William I of England.

The whole story of the invasion is shown in great detail in the **Bayeux Tapestry**, or the **Tapestry of Queen Matilda**, as it is known in France. It is more than **230ft (70m)** long with **58** scenes. It was commissioned by the Bishop of Bayeux for his new cathedral between 1066 and 1077. It is supposed to have been designed in Canterbury and made by English needlewomen.

Plan of landing beaches at Arromanches

The invasion of Normandy – 'Operation Overlord'

In May-June 1940 the Germans invaded France. Soon Paris was taken. By 1942 the tide of war had turned and the allies planned the invasion of France.

The first attempt was the Dieppe raid, which was a disaster – almost 5,000 out of a force of 7,000 men, mostly Canadians, were killed or captured. But Dieppe provided valuable lessons. The northern ports were very strongly defended; to ensure surprise the attack would have to be made further west, using mobile port facilities.

D-Day – June 6th 1944

325,000 men in 5,000 boats landed on the coast of Normandy. The six weeks that followed saw some of the fiercest fighting of the war. One village changed hands 20 times in two weeks. 200,000 buildings were destroyed and some 600 villages had to be rebuilt after the war. Supplies were landed from England on the Mulberries – prefabricated harbours floated across the Channel. One was installed on **Arromanches** beach, where the British forces landed.

Eventually a million men took part in the invasion – Americans, British and Commonwealth troops and the Free French Army under General Leclerc.

The history of Normandy is not entirely devoted to war. In the middle ages Norman architecture developed a magnificent style of its own which preceded the Gothic style. The fortified **Abbey of Mont Saint Michel** is one of the finest examples of Gothic building.

Appeal for freedom

On June 18 1940, **General de Gaulle** made his famous appeal on BBC radio: "France has lost a battle, but not the war". From London he led the **Free French** forces, and in 1944 the Free French took part in the Normandy landings. Symbolically they were the first to enter Paris. Hitler had ordered the destruction of the city. But mines placed on the main buildings were never detonated.

BBC copyright photograph

Extra Extra Extra Extra

☆☆Make a list of foods and drinks for which Normandy is famous.

☆☆Name 4 cities in Normandy.

☆☆What sort of weapon killed Harold at the Battle of Hastings?

Ile-de-France
Birthplace of Gothic architecture

Romanesque style

Between the 10th and 13th centuries there were two revolutions in building techniques. The first produced the **Romanesque** style, the second the **Gothic** style.

A wide variety of Romanesque churches were built all over France. Instead of roofing them with wooden beams, which were

Louis IX, known as Saint Louis (1226-1270).
People came from all over France, bringing their legal problems to him. He would hear their cases sitting under an oak tree in the park of his château at Vincennes, now a Paris suburb.

a fire hazard, the builders used an ancient Roman technique of **rounded stone arches** with **strong square towers.**

But the Romanesque arch has one great disadvantage – it is very heavy, requiring **thick walls** and buttresses, allowing only **tiny windows.** The buildings are therefore very dark.

Gothic style

Then, from the Ile-de-France in the north came a new architecture, much disapproved of by the Romanesque builders, who called it **GOTHIC** meaning **barbaric.** But the Gothic style was to spread all over Europe.

Gothic buildings are much higher with much larger windows. The builders managed this by using **pointed arches** and vaults supported by **very thin stone ribs.** Gothic churches have **tall pointed spires** and beautiful stained glass windows.

The Gothic style spread fast and soon many rich cities were building cathedrals. Often the whole population of the city would be involved in the work. Young and old, rich and poor often laboured without wages, pleased to help in the building of a holy place. The work took years. The famous **cathedral** at **Chartres,** which has one Romanesque tower and one Gothic tower, contains **1,800 sculptures** and took **30 years** to build.

Romanesque and Gothic

Visiting churches and cathedrals can be made more interesting if you can recognise some basic styles. Look out for:

Romanesque
Rounded arches
Dog-toothed, geometric designs
Strong square towers
Small windows and dark interiors

Gothic
Tall thin spires
Pointed arches
High, vaulted roofs, flying buttresses

Lightness and delicacy of the clustered pillars
Large lofty windows with beautiful stained glass

Right: *Reims cathedral — with its 2,000 statues and immense lacework of stone is one of the most richly decorated in France.*

Below right: *The first major Gothic church was the* **Abbey of Saint-Denis,** *near Paris. The Romanesque influence on the building is still very strong. It contains the tombs of all the kings of France. Saint Denis is said to have walked there carrying his head after being beheaded at Montmartre.*

Some of the most famous Romanesque churches are in:
Autun, Vezelay, Caen, Poitiers, Saint Nectaire, Arles, Toulouse.

Some of the most famous Gothic churches are in:
Paris (Saint-Denis, Notre-Dame), Chartres, Beauvais, Reims, Amiens, Auxerre, Rouen, Bourges, Le Mans.

Champagne

Dom Pérignon's discovery

Until the end of the 17th century the wines of Champagne were flat. The normal process of the fermentation of wine produces gas, which is allowed to escape into the air. It is only possible to make wine bubble if it ferments in the bottle, trapping the gas. Three hundred years ago bottles did not have air-tight seals.

In 1688 Dom Pérignon was appointed monk in charge of wine at the monastery of **Hautvilliers** near Reims. He had learned from Spanish monks how cork could seal bottles – just what he needed to perfect sparkling wines. His invention has become a world-famous industry.

Deep beneath the chalk hills of Champagne are over 200 miles of cellars. The chalk keeps them constantly at exactly the right temperature (10°C, 50°F) for storing the bottles. If the temperature changes sud-

Early morning Vendange, on the banks of the River Marne.

denly, the bottles are liable to explode.

Only a very small area around **Reims** and **Epernay** has the right to call its wine **Champagne**.

The Champagne Fairs

In the middle ages the two richest parts of Europe were **Flanders** and **Northern Italy**. Cities like **Ypres** and **Ghent** in Flanders were centres of the wool and textile industries. **Genoa, Pisa** and **Venice** in Italy were trading ports, whose merchants imported silks, spices, jewellery and dyes from as far east as India.

Champagne had the great advantage of being about half way between Flanders and Italy. The region was efficiently and peacefully ruled by its Counts. Every year there were six trade fairs in Champagne.

Each fair lasted for six weeks or more, so there was an almost permanent bustle of activity. Different areas of the towns specialised in different trades –

horses in one place, **land, leather, hemp** (for ropes), **dried fish, sugar, paper, weapons, ceramics** and banking services in others.

Cities like **Troyes** became very rich, building a cathedral on the profits. But by the end of the 13th century the fairs began to decline. Inflation and the beginning of the Hundred Years' War made trade dangerous. New shipbuilding methods made sea transport easier than land routes with pack animals.

A stall at one of the Foires de Champagne.

This picture, taken from a Tapestry of the life of St Remi shows him hading over a barrel of Champagne wine to King Clovis.

Annointing the kings

In the cathedral of the capital of Champagne, **Reims**, French kings were crowned for hundreds of years.

In AD 507 **Clovis,** the first king of what is now France, was converted to Christianity with his entire victorious army. **St Remi,** archbishop of Reims, is supposed to have baptised Clovis with holy oil brought down from heaven by a dove.

Languedoc

The name **Languedoc** comes from the language, the **Langue d'Oc,** which was spoken throughout southern France. In the north the **Langue d'Oil** was spoken. So different were the languages that the 14th century French Popes had to have the king of France's letters translated. The differences between the south (called the **Midi**) and the north go back to Roman times. But the crusade against the Cathars allowed the northerners to take over the south completely. The **Langue d'Oc** declined and the region became poor.

The Roman arena at Arles

The Cathars
In the 11th century a religious sect called the **Cathars,** or **Albingensians,** sprang up in the south west of France. Their leaders were called the **parfaits** (perfect ones).

They lived lives of poverty and purity in protest against corruption among priests and church leaders. They were Christians but not of the official church.

Pope Innocent III launched a crusade against them as heretics. Special Inquisition courts were set up to try the Cathars. Torture was used. Punishments varied from prison and pilgrimage to burning at the stake. Those who survived had to wear yellow crosses sewn onto their clothes.

In one village a woman had her tongue cut out for accusing the local priest of being a Cathar. Later the priest himself was arrested as a heretic and died in prison. On another occasion a whole village was arrested (except for children under 12) for not paying taxes to the church. It was not until a century later that the last of the Cathars were subdued.

The walled city of Carcassonne

Carcassonne
Today the walled city of Carcassonne looks more or less as it did in the 12th century. During the crusade against the Cathars in 1209, the city was besieged. After only two weeks traitors let the crusaders in. The city and the surrounding countryside were ravaged. It was many years before the townspeople were allowed to rebuild their homes, and then not behind the walls. The ruins of the 52 towers were used as stone quarries for hundreds of years.

By the 19th century very little remained. Then, on the orders of Napoleon III the famous architect, Viollet-le-Duc, undertook the enormous project of restoring the city to its former magnificence.

Toulouse
Toulouse, known as the **Ville Rose** because of the warm pink of the city's brick and stone in the sunlight, was once the capital of independent Languedoc. The region was rich and cultured. **Troubadours,** wandering poets, sang elegant love songs in beautiful cities like **Toulouse** and **Carcassonne.** All this was destroyed by the crusaders. Toulouse became little more than an agricultural town. Today it is best known as the centre of the aircraft industry. Concorde was built nearby.

The city of Toulouse

Burgundy

Burgundy is rich in history, art, architecture, food and wine. Burgundians have always lived well and enjoyed life.

In the Hundred Years' War the dukes frequently sided with the English against the French King. They allowed the English into Paris in 1418 and sold Joan of Arc to them in 1430.

Life in the monasteries
Medieval monasteries were not only religious organisations. They were also trading houses, banks and industrial concerns. The monks built roads, arranged mortgages and received vast donations of land. They became wealthy and influential.

The first attempt at reform was the foundation of the **Abbey of Cluny** in 911. But soon Cluny became extremely rich, building an Abbey that was the largest church in Christendom, until the construction of Saint Peter's in Rome.

Specialities of the south coast:
Bouillabaisse — fish stew
Pissaladière — savoury tart
Ratatouille — tomatoes, green peppers and aubergines dish
Aioli — mayonnaise with garlic

In 1098 a group of reformers gathered at **Citeaux,** starting the strict **Cistercian** order. The monks had one meal a day, with no meat, eggs or fish. They worked for 12 hours a day, beginning at 2am with matins. The next service was at dawn. Then they laboured in the fields until the middle of the afternoon. The day ended with vespers.

But after the death of their founder, Saint Bernard, the Cistercians, too, grew rich and worldly. Burgundy, with its rich agriculture and trade routes to Italy, made fortunes for the monks at the expense of their principles.

The Hospices de Beaune

The rich Burgundians were great patrons of the arts. As Flanders was part of Burgundy, Flemish masters like **Van Eyck** painted for them. **Van der Weyden** painted his famous **Last Judgment** for Nicholas Rolin when he founded the **Hospice de Beaune** in 1443.

The Hospice, a home for the elderly, still looks after old people and orphans and still contains Van der Weyden's picture. Now, as in the middle ages, Burgundy grows much of what is best in French produce – **Charolais beef, Dijon mustard** and good quality red wine.

Orléans and Rouen

Jeanne d'Arc

Joan of Arc was born in the village of **Domrémy** in **Lorraine,** north eastern France. The population of the village is only a few hundred, but thousands of tourists make their way there every year to see the birthplace of **La Pucelle, the Maid of Orleans.** Joan of Arc has become a national heroine, with plays, sculptures and paintings dedicated to her.

Joan belonged to a peasant family. Her father was fairly prosperous, owning a farm outside the village. At the age of 13 she became very religious and spent a lot of time meditating and praying alone. Other girls in the village thought she was almost too devoted to God.

After meditating for some time, Joan began to express great concern about the war with the English, who had occupied large parts of France (the Hundred Years' War). She claimed she could hear heavenly voices and that she could see visions of saint Margaret, saint Catherine and the archangel Michael, patron saint of soldiers. She said the voices told her to lead the French troops to victory against the English.

Much of France was under English occupation during the Hundred Years' War, and with difficulty Joan managed to get permission to cross parts of this territory. She made the dangerous journey to the River **Loire,** at **Chinon,** to see **Charles VII** – the still uncrowned king of France.

Charles believed her story enough to provide her with troops. In May 1429 came the turning point of the war. Clad in armour, holding the banner of France, Joan set out to lead her troops to free the town of **Orléans** from the English! After four days of fighting Joan, still not yet 17, emerged victorious!

Her next dream was also to be fulfilled as she saw **Charles VII** annointed king in **Reims** cathedral.

Joan then felt her job was finished and wanted to go back home. But Charles persuaded her to help him in his fight against the Burgundians. This battle she did not win. She was taken prisoner by the Burgundians, who sold her to the English as a prize of war.

The English took her in chains to **Rouen** and kept her prisoner for months, before they tried her for witchcraft and heresy.

Deserted by her voices, her king and the people she saved, she defended herself at the trial bravely and eloquently, but she was found guilty.

Her sentence was death by fire at the stake. She was burned alive in the **Place du Vieux Marché,** Rouen on **May 30 1431.**

Joan had saved France from the English, but it took a long time for her to become the national heroine she is today.

The Church rehabilitated her in 1456, but she was not made a saint until 1920, when another foreign power, this time **Germany,** occupied her native Lorraine.

This plaque reads:
Joan of Arc, prisoner of the English, was taken to Saint-Valéry-sur-Somme in December 1430

La Place du Vieux Marche, Rouen, where Joan was burnt to death in 1431

La Fête de Jeanne d'Arc, celebrated in Orléans, the town she won back for France

Joan of Arc, in Domrémy, hears the voices of saints telling her to save France from the English

The châteaux of the Loire

The château of Chenonceaux
Originally built by a rich financier, the château passed to Henry II, who gave it as a present to Diane de Poitiers. More than 2,000 wounded Frenchmen were cared for there during the First World War. Later the château was bought by the chocolate manufacturer, **Menier.**

In the 15th century the Loire valley was a region which French nobles and courtiers had come to know very well. This was because most of the rest of France was occupied by the English at this time. The court and nobles often had to leave Paris.

The mild weather and the great hunting forests of the Loire made it an ideal place for sumptuous royal residences. And so fashionable elaborate **châteaux** were built there.

But the châteaux were not to be used for defence purposes. They would be useless against armies now supplied with cannon. Instead they were built as beautiful country houses.

They were decorated in the style of the **Italian Renaissance,** which was to change the art, architecture and learning of the whole of Europe.

The châteaux were adorned with magnificent works of art. **Leonardo da Vinci** painted the **Mona Lisa** for Francois I. Leonardo died at Amboise on the River Loire.

The most beautiful woman in France

The most celebrated beauty of the age was **Diane de Poitiers.** She was the mistress of two kings in succession. A widow in her early thirties, she was first mistress of **Francois I** and then of his son **Henry II.**

She was 20 years older than Henry, but he adored her. He gave her lavish presents such as title deeds to castles, and once even dropped the crown jewels into her lap.

He also gave her a present of the **château of Chenonceaux,** where she frequently lived with both Henry and his wife **Catherine de Médicis.** Diane even nursed Catherine through an attack of scarlet fever!

The château of Chenonceaux lies on a tributary of the Loire, called the River **Cher.** It was Diane who connected the **château** to the opposite bank of the Cher, by having

---

We three kings

Three outsize characters dominated Europe at the beginning of the 16th century – **Francois I,** King of France, **Henry VIII,** King of England and **Charles V,** King of Spain and Holy Roman Emperor.

There was great rivalry between the monarchs, both on and off the battlefield. Henry and Francois vied with each other to have the more magnificent court.

Francois was proud, extravagant, impetuous, ambitious and a lover of the arts. He built the beautiful châteaux of Chambord on the Loire and Fontainebleau near Paris. Great artists like Leonardo da Vinci, Cellini and Titian visited his court.

Henry was a great archer, tennis player, wrestler, linguist and musician. One day he asked an Italian visitor if Francois was as tall as he was, or as stout. He even asked about his legs and, as the reply came that Francois' legs were 'spare', he showed off his own for all to see how shapely they were.

---

the bridge built.

It was, however, Henry's wife, **Catherine,** who had the famous gallery built on the bridge, after the death of her husband.

Henry was killed in a jousting accident in 1559 and Catherine took Chenonceaux away from Diane de Poitiers, giving her the nearby château of **Chaumont** instead.

Even at the age of 60 Diane was said to be the most beautiful woman in France.

Versailles

A château as lavish as Versailles could only have been built by the king of the richest and most powerful nation in Europe. In the 17th century the population of France was some 18 million, about three times that of England. Such was the extravagance of **Louis XIV** that building and decorating the palace and its gardens crippled the national treasury. The site was most unsuitable, with deep marshes but no running water. The ground had to be drained and levelled. Water was brought in for the fountains and pools, of which **460** still exist.

By isolating his nobles at Versailles, away from their lands and from Paris, Louis was able to keep complete control over them.

Louis XIV became known as the '**Sun King**' and he could rightly proclaim, '**L'Etat, c'est moi**', (**I am the State**).

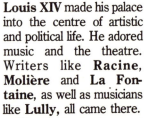

Louis XIV made his palace into the centre of artistic and political life. He adored music and the theatre. Writers like **Racine**, **Molière** and **La Fontaine**, as well as musicians like **Lully**, all came there.

The king's day began at about noon, with breakfast. Lunch was in the late afternoon and dinner at about midnight. He lived entirely in public. He ate (in enormous quantities), went to bed, got up and ruled the kingdom in front of crowds of the **20,000 people** who thronged the palace.

Fashions changed constantly, with Louis leading the way. Wigs became popular after about 1670, when he began to go bald! Their wigs were never properly cleaned, becoming so dirty that mice made their homes in them!

Under **Louis XV** the grand state rooms of Versailles continued to be used for court ceremonies, but this king preferred to live in smaller, more comfortable apartments. In the park he built much smaller palaces called **Trianons**. **Marie Antoinette**, wife of **Louis XVI**, went one further and built a hamlet in the gardens where she played at being a shepherdess. She was a selfish spendthrift and as a result extremely unpopular. When told that the people had no bread, she is supposed to have said, '**Let them eat brioche**' (cake). She was executed during the Revolution.

Above: *The hamlet of Marie Antoinette*

The famous **Hall of Mirrors** at Versailles has played an important part in French history. At the end of the war between France and Prussia in 1871, the German Chancellor, **Bismarck**, announced the creation of the German Empire from the **Galerie des Glaces**. The French had their revenge at the **Treaty of Versailles** which ended World War I in 1918, imposing very harsh conditions on Germany contributing to World War II.

Building Versailles

1661 Work began and was to last for almost **30 years**.
22,000 men and **6,000** horses were employed on the project.
Le Nòtre designed the gardens.
Le Brun designed the interiors.

1678–1684 Construction of the Hall of Mirrors.

1682 Louis XIV officially moved in to Versailles. But the Palace was still a building site. Courtiers found themselves stepping through the mud.

1685 Over 30,000 men still working at Versailles. Many workers died. Every night cartloads of bodies were carried away. In the gardens there were eventually 1,400 fountains and 2,000 statues.

1689 Versailles was finished. But already the kingdom was in serious financial difficulty. Louis XIV's wars and Versailles had crippled the national treasury.
The only thing Louis did not spend money on was the heating. Apparently he never felt the cold and always had the windows open. Contemporary accounts say that in winter wine would freeze in the glasses.

Paris – The French Revolution, 1789

The French Revolution was a turning point in world history. Until then nobles owned most of the land in Europe and ordinary people had no say in the affairs of government. Before the revolution broke out in 1789, writers had been devising new ideas about political freedom and equality between classes.

Before the revolution nobles and French clergy owned 80 per cent of the land, while many peasants starved.

For 15 years Paris was the centre of almost continuous revolution.

After this the slogan of the French revolutionaries, **Liberté, Egalité, Fraternité**, was taken up by nationalists and radicals all over Europe.

La prise de la Bastille – 14 juillet, 1789
July 14, *(La Fête Nationale) celebrates the storming of the Bastille Prison in Paris in 1789. The Bastille had symbolised the oppressive hand of royal government.*

The execution of Louis XVI – 1793

At his coronation in 1754 Louis XVI complained that his crown was uncomfortable. Thirty years later during the French revolution, he was to find his position as king far more uncomfortable.

Louis could never accept that he was no longer an all-powerful king. He ruled indecisively and even tried to escape, but he was caught near the frontier and dragged back to Paris.

He was thrown into jail and later, in January **1793,** he was executed in the Place Louis XV, now known as the **Place de la Concorde.** His coach was taken through the Paris streets for two hours before the execution, preceded by drummers to drown any cries of 'Long live the King'. He courageously protested when the three executioners tried to take off his coat and tie his hands. He shouted out that he was innocent and forgave his executioners.

Nine months later **Marie Antoinette**, his Queen, was guillotined, too. Their eldest son, the **Dauphin**, disappeared in jail.

Altogether 2,800 people were executed in the Place de la Concorde during the revolution. From time to time the guillotine had to be moved to allow the blood to be washed away.

Napoleon Bonaparte

As a boy in **Corsica Napoleon Bonaparte** won a scholarship to study in France. At 17 he was in military college and at 20, when the revolution broke out, he was an army lieutenant. At 24 he was a general. After several military campaigns, he returned to Paris and took power in November **1799**. He made himself the virtual dictator of France.

After years of revolutionary disorder, Napoleon organised the government with military efficiency. He made peace with the Church, reorganised taxes and made a code of laws out of the confused mass of revolutionary reforms. In 1804 he made himself **Emperor** of France.

His invasion plans against England were frustrated by the English command of the sea, emphasised by the French defeat at **Trafalgar** in 1805. But on land he defeated one European power after another: The Austrians at **Austerlitz** (1805), the Prussians at **Jena** (1806) and the Russians at **Friedland** (1807).

By **1812**, when he occupied **Moscow**, Napoleon controlled Europe from Portugal to Russia. But already the tide was turning. In 1814 Paris was captured and Napoleon exiled to the **island of Elba**. A year later he was back in Paris. But he was defeated at **Waterloo** by the Prussians and English and again exiled – this time to remote **St Helena** in the Atlantic, where he died in **1821** aged **52**.

Les Invalides *was built as a home for the veterans of* **Louis XIV's** *many wars. But today it is best known because it houses* **Napoleon's tomb.**

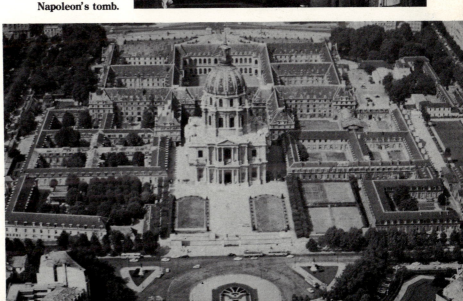

Paris – The modern city

Montmartre

In the early 19th century Montmartre was still a country village, surrounded by vineyards, farms and windmills. Artists from Paris came there because it was picturesque and provided cheap lodging. Soon it became the centre of the 'bohemian life' with cabarets like the famous Moulin Rouge (Red Windmill), where they danced the can-can.

The Commune

In 1871 Montmartre was the centre of the last great

To expiate the crimes of the Commune, 'the workers' revolt of 1871, the Catholic Church decided to build the present **basilica of the Sacré Coeur** *(Sacred Heart) in 1873.*

Parisian revolution. Paris had been besieged by the Germans through a winter of bombardment and famine.

The French government surrendered to the Germans, but the Commune (the City Council) of Paris organised the first genuine workers' revolt in history. From Versailles the official government directed a civil war. Over 30,000 of the Communards (supporters of the Commune) were shot before the struggle ended.

Today Montmartre retains its artistic traditions. The **Place du Tertre** is full of artists, painting among other traditional subjects, the 'poulbot', the urchin.

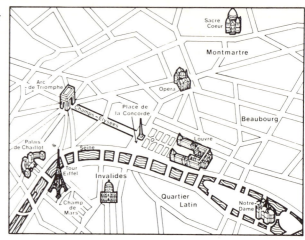

The tomb of the Unknown Soldier

On November 11, 1920, two years after the armistice which ended the First World War, the body of an unknown soldier was solemnly laid to rest under the Arc de Triomphe. He lies under a simple stone, which bears this inscription: **'Here lies a French soldier who died for his country 1914–1918'.** A flame which never goes out, night or day, burns at his head, as a symbol of gratitude to those who died.

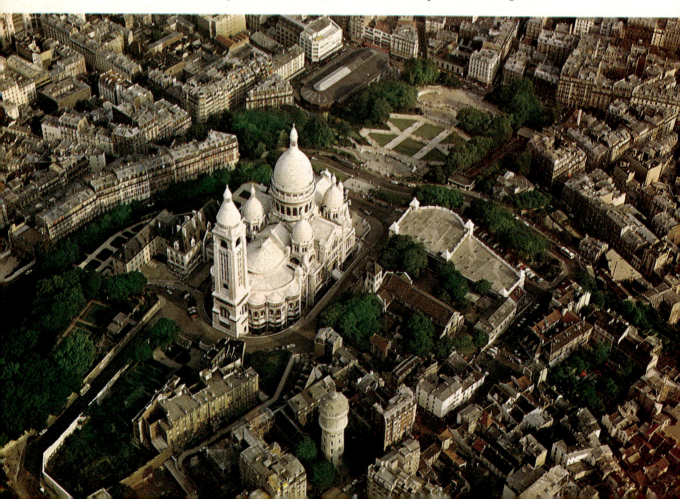

President Georges Pompidou left his mark on Paris with two enormous building projects – **Les Halles** and the **Beaubourg**. **Les Halles**, the old Paris market, known as the 'Belly of Paris', was moved to a new site outside the city. This left a vast hole, which no one seemed to know what to do with. Eventually it was filled with a commercial centre below street level and new underground railway station. Not far away the **Centre Georges Pompidou**, otherwise known as the Beaubourg, has been a greater success. It was designed by an Englishman and is known as the 'oil refinery', because of the brightly coloured pipes all over the outside. Inside there is a library, a museum of modern art and exhibition halls. Outside there are always street performers and players.

L'Etoile
The building of the Arc de Triomphe was begun by **Napoleon** on his birthday, **August 15 1806**. It was not completed until **1836**. The **Place de l'Etoile** surrounding the Arc de Triomphe was officially re-christened the **Place Charles de Gaulle** in 1970, but Parisians still call it the **Etoile** (star).

The Centre Beaubourg

Les événements de mai '68
The month of May 1968 proved that the tradition of Parisian revolutions is not dead. In a period of apparent political and economic calm a series of violent encounters between police and students erupted in the **Latin Quarter**, the traditional student area of Paris. The troubles had begun at the **University of Nanterre** in the suburbs, with demands for a fundamental reform of the whole university system. On May 3 the Sorbonne University in Paris was closed by the authorities. A month of street fighting followed.

The CRS, the riot police, were armed with steel helmets, shields, CS gas and water cannon. The students fought with **Pavés** (paving stones) and barricades built from cars, buses and fallen trees. The trouble spread to the factories. Many workers went on strike. The Government almost fell. But negotiations ended the troubles and de Gaulle was confirmed in office by an election. Only a year later he resigned and was replaced by Georges Pompidou.

Lourdes

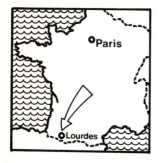

In February 1858 a 14 year old girl, **Bernadette Soubirous**, claimed to have seen a vision of the Virgin Mary in a cave at Lourdes in the French Pyrenees. Bernadette maintained the Virgin appeared to her 18 times. On one of these occasions water spurted from a rock and a spring, which had never been seen before,

German members of an international soldiers' pilgrimage to Lourdes

flowed from the spot. Soon many people believed stories of the miraculous power of the water to heal sickness. Pilgrimages began and in 1933 Bernadette was made a saint. Some three million pilgrims from all over the world go to Lourdes every year. Many of them are sick.

While religious practice has declined over the last hundred years, the importance of Lourdes has grown enormously. In 1958, to celebrate the centenary of the vision of Sainte Bernadette the largest underground church in the world was built there. Although pilgrims visit Lourdes all the year round, the main festivities take place on **August 25**, when thousands of people join daylight and torchlight processions to the Grotto.

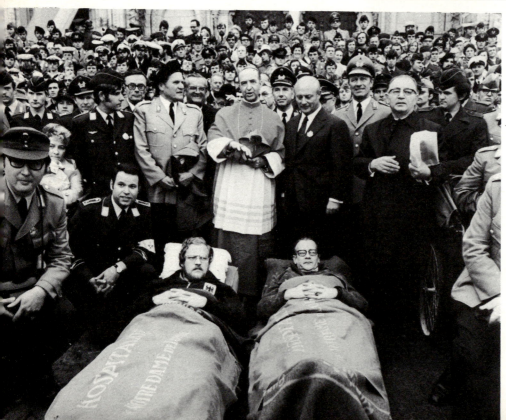

France is basically a Roman Catholic country. In the 16th century there was a succession of wars between Catholics and Protestants, ended by the **Edict of Nantes**, which allowed religious freedom to both. But **Louis XIV**, known as the **'Most Christian King'** as well as the **'Sun King'**, revoked the Edict and sent Protestants to the galleys. Many fled to England. By the time of the Revolution (1789) the Catholic Church was rich and corrupt.

Picardy

France is protected by natural frontiers of mountains and sea, *except* in the north east. For centuries this has been the route taken by invaders. Even conquerors of Roman Gaul came this way. Calais was captured by the English at the beginning of the Hundred Years' War.

The First World War – 1914–1918

In **August 1914** the Germans invaded France. By September they were near Paris and the government took refuge at Bordeaux. The French and British launched a counter attack, forcing the Germans back.

British troops exhausted in the trenches.

The stalemate of trench warfare was to last four years with very heavy casualties. By the end of the first *year* the French had lost 300,000 men with 600,000 wounded.

The trenches in which the men fought, ate and slept were often only **two feet** (60cm) wide. But they were **six feet** (2m) or more deep, often flooded and infested with rats. The lines of enemy trenches were only about **100yds** (90m) away and sometimes as close as **25yds** (22m). The soldiers were covered in lice and from 1916 onwards suffered gas attacks as well.

When they went into action the loss of life was appalling. In the three and a half month long **Battle of Verdun** (1916) the French and Germans lost 700,000 men between them. Altogether the war claimed **1.8 million German, 1.3 million French** and almost **1 million British lives**.

The people of northern France have a reputation for hard work, courage and patriotism. At the beginning of the

Hundred Years' War the English captured Calais after a siege lasting a year. **King Edward III** demanded that seven citizens, in their shirts, with ropes round their necks, should bring him the keys of the city. The Queen was so impressed with the courage and dignity of the **Burghers** (prominent citizens), who expected to be hanged, that she persuaded Edward to release them. The French sculptor **Rodin** made a famous statue of the Burghers, which stands outside **Calais Town Hall**. A copy stands next to the **House of Lords** in London.

Extra Extra Extra Extra

☆☆British troops fought in the famous Battle of the Somme. Find the river Somme on a map of France.

☆☆Find out which province was returned to France in 1918 after German occupation.

☆☆Give the dates of the Second World War.

Alsace-Lorraine

Situated on the German border this province has seen many bitter conflicts between France and Germany. Many of the towns have German sounding names – Mulhouse, Altkirch, Ottmarsheim. Both countries have been anxious to own the area for more than sentimental reasons. It is rich in **iron-ore** and **coal**.

Until recently the large natural deposits and industrial development in Lorraine made it one of the most prosperous parts of France. But today there are signs that the industry has become outdated. Many people have been put out of work in steel mill closures.

Général de Gaulle took the double **Cross of Lorraine** as his symbol during the Second World War.

Strasbourg

Above: The name Strasbourg means 'city at the cross-roads'. Strasbourg has changed nationality four times in a century. Perhaps because of this, the city is now a symbol of European unity — the meeting place of the European parliament.

Right: The city contains many examples of these fine timbered houses built in the Middle Ages.

Choucroute, *the famous dish from Alsace, is like the German Sauerkraut, or pickled cabbage. The wines of Alsace (***Riesling, Moselle)*** as well as its beers, are very similar to the German drinks. The Alsatians are allowed to add sugar to their wines, a practice not allowed in the rest of France, but common in Germany.*

Extra Extra

☆☆Joan of Arc lived in a tiny village in Lorraine. Find out its name.

☆☆Name 4 cities in Alsace-Lorraine.

☆☆A famous French song begins: **En passant par la Lorraine, avec mes sabots...** Find out what **sabots** are.

☆☆Another famous French song was written in Strasbourg by **Rouget de Lisle.** What is it?

Auvergne

Six hundred million years ago the Auvergne was part of a continuous chain of mountains stretching from **Cornwall**, through **Brittany**, down to the **Massif Central** and back north towards **Belgium**. Volcanoes erupted when the Alps were being pushed up against the Massif Central. As a result the Auvergne now has a harsh landscape of extinct volcanoes and poor soil.

The people have always been poor, with a reputation for meanness, like that of the Scots. In spite of this, the region produced one of the most advanced civilisations of Gaul. The last two Presidents of France, **Valéry Giscard d'Estaing** and **Georges Pompidou**, both came from the area.

Below: La Chaîne des Puys

The first national hero

Vercingétorix is the most famous Auvergnat. He was a leader of the people who lived in the region in Roman times. He has become a national hero in France, because of the way he tried to unite the **Gauls** against the Romans. Vercingétorix almost captured Gaul from **Caesar**, who wrote about the bravery and intelligence of his enemies, the **Gauls**. But eventually Caesar defeated them at **Alesia**. **Vercingétorix** was taken to Rome and exhibited in a triumphal procession, before being strangled in prison.

Above: Vichy France and Marshal Pétain

The Vichy government

During the **Second World War Vichy**, a small spa town in the Auvergne, was briefly the capital of France. When the French government collapsed before the German invasion in **1940**, the country was divided into two parts. The **north** was occupied directly by the **Germans**. The **south** was governed from **Vichy** in collaboration with the Germans by **Marshal Pétain**. He was then 84 and a hero of the First World War. With the allied invasion of 1944, Pétain fled to Switzerland. Later he returned to France to be tried for collaborating with the Germans. In spite of his age he was sent to prison, where he died in 1951, aged 91.

Region by Region Quiz

A

Tick the correct answers

1 **The storming of the Bastille prison in Paris took place**
   a. in May 1968 ☐
   b. on July 14 1789. ☐
   c. on November 11 1918. ☐

* * *

2 **During the revolution of 1789 the guillotine was set up in**
   a. the Place de la Concorde. ☐
   b. the Place de l'Etoile. ☐
   c. Les Halles. ☐

3 **The tombs built by prehistoric people in Brittany are called**
   a. pardons ☐
   b. dolmens ☐
   c. menhirs ☐

* * *

4 **Louis XIV built Versailles because**
   a. he wanted to keep all his nobles under his power and in one place. ☐
   b. the site was suitable for a château. ☐
   c. he had too much money and wanted to spend some. ☐

Place de la Concorde, Paris

The Chateau of Versailles with statue of Louis XIV

5 **During the Hundred Years' War, Joan of Arc liberated the town of**
   a. Rouen ☐
   b. Chinon ☐
   c. Orléans ☐
   d. Paris ☐

The statue of Joan of Arc

Paris, Le Louvre

B

Finish off these sentences. The correct answers are jumbled up opposite.

The gardens at Versailles

1 The Centre Beaubourg in Paris was built for ....
The Arc de Triomphe was built for ....
The Place de la Concorde was built for ....

Bonaparte

Pompidou

Louis XV

* * *

2 The little hameau at Versailles was built for ....
The birth of the German Empire was announced from the Hall of Mirrors at Versailles by ....
The Gardens at Versailles were designed by ....
The Palace of Versailles was built for ....

Le Nôtre

Marie Antoinette

Bismarck

Louis XIV

3 Joan of Arc was born in ....
She saved the town of ....
She had the king crowned in .
She was burned alive in ....

Rouen
Domrémy
Reims
Orléans

4 The D-Day landings in World War II took place in ....
The city of Strasbourg is in ..
The Hospices de Beaune are in ....
The walled town of Carcassonne is in ....

Languedoc

Burgundy

Alsace-Lorraine

Normandy

Extra Extra Extra Extra Extra Extra Extra Extra

Questions involving further research

1 Which armed forces took part in the **Normandy landings** in 1944?

2 Why was a French government set up in 1940 at **Vichy** in the Auvergne? How long did it last?

3 What are the reasons for the quality and rarity of **Champagne** wines?

4 What are the hopes of the sick people who go to **Lourdes**?

5 Why were **Marshal Pétain** and **General de Gaulle** so divided during the Second World War?

6 List the main differences between **Gothic** and **Romanesque** architecture.

(You'll find most of the answers on pages 58-77)

Settling in

Most and least

To whom did you speak **most** French?

What surprised you **most** about the place you stayed in?

Which meal did you enjoy **most**? Write out your favourite menu in French in your note book.

Which foods surprised you the **most**?

Which dish would you **most** like to see available in Britain?

What did you like **least** about the place you stayed in?

What was the **least** enjoyable dish you tried?

Which was the **least** successful part of your trip? Why do you think it was so?

Above: *Mont Saint-Michel*
Above right: *Sailing lessons in Saint Cast*
Right: *Mont Saint-Michel*

Work out the hidden message. Unscramble the words. Take the triangle first, then the squares, then the circles, then the diamonds.

Bibendum – the Michelin Man

Where did he come from?

At the Lyons exhibition of 1889 Michelin had a stand displaying the tyres for which they had become so famous.

The inventors of these tyres, André and Edouard Michelin arrived at their stand, and here they found that the stand manager had stacked them in assorted sizes. This sight fired the imagination of Édouard. He remarked "If it had arms it would look like a man". Little did he realise that this innocent remark was to create one of the world's most famous trade marks.

Some while after this, André was visited by a Monsieur O'Galop, who had come to show him some sketches for advertisements. While looking among them, André caught sight of a cartoon of a fat man raising his beer mug and announcing

Nunc est Bibendum – Now is the time to drink

André immediately thought of what his brother had said at Lyons and he told O'Galop.

In no time the tyre man replaced the robust drinker and the beer mug was replaced by a champagne glass full of nails and broken glass.

What is his name?

The first poster on which the rotund Michelin man came to life was when he stood at a banqueting table flanked by two flattened competitors. Lifting his glass he toasted

Nunc est Bibendum – Your good health; Michelin tyres swallow obstacles

He was finally christened **Bibendum** by the racing driver Théry, who on seeing André Michelin go by called out "Look, there is **Bibendum**".

Although born without legs, they were soon to appear, for **Bibendum** had caught the imagination of the artists. He became instantly human, with the stroke of a pen he walked, danced, jumped and ran, he laughed, cried, became angry, pensive and tender. With his new personality **Bibendum** became the leading actor in every kind of Michelin publicity.

On the road

We're on our way home after a holiday in Brittany. Almost home.... but.... oh dear... I wish we were better at map reading! See if you can do any better!

Which towns are these?

Unscramble the names. They are all on the map.

NACE

SILIXUE

RIVE

TTTEERA

EILLVUAED

EFPAMC

EL RAHVE

Extra Extra

(The clues are all road numbers on the map.)

Name the French port at which the famous World War 2 Normandy landings were made. (Clue D514)

Find the names of 2 towns famous for the cheeses made there. (Clue – look on roads numbered D4 and N815)

Find the name of the town in which the liqueur BENEDICTINE is made. (Clue D940)

For what is the town of BAYEUX (N13) famous?

1 The Légourd family is heading for ÉTRETAT. Can you find it on the map? It's by the sea and not too far from LE HAVRE.

2 The map shows a part of which region in France?
   a. The Auvergne   b. Champagne   c. Normandy

3 LE HAVRE is a big Channel port. From Le Havre you can sail by ferry to a big English port. Which is it?
   a. Dover   b. Southampton   c. Ramsgate

4 What is the popular French name for the motorway A 13?
   a. L'Aquitaine   b. L'Autoroute du Soleil   c. L'Autoroute de Normandie

5 The A 13 goes from CAEN to . . .
   a. Paris   b. Lisieux   c. Le Havre

6 Follow these directions. In which towns will you end up?
   Leave LE HAVRE by the D940. At ÉTRETAT, take the D11.
   Go through YPORT and you arrive at ?
   Leave CAEN by the D22. At BAYEUX take the D516 to ?
   From ST LÔ take the D972, then the D572 to BAYEUX. Go on to the dual carriageway
   N13 and drive 27 kilometres to ?

Quiz?? Quiz?? Quiz?? Quiz??

The answers to these quiz questions are all jumbled up at the bottom of the page. Try to answer them without looking first.

1 Passing through the customs, cars must display one of two signs, indicating whether the passengers have 'nothing to declare' or 'goods to declare'. In French 'nothing to declare' is RIEN À DECLARER. What is the French for 'goods to declare'?

NOTHING TO DECLARE
(IF THE CAR IS INSURED)

RIEN A DECLARER

GOODS TO DECLARE

?

2 If you have nothing to declare do you display the green sticker or the red one?

3 What colour are the road signs on the autoroutes in France?

4 Where would you see the initial letters of these words TRANSIT INTERNATIONAL ROUTIER? The words concern an international customs agreement.

5 What is the French for coach?

6 In France you saw that the roads were named A N, D or C roads. Which letter represents the most minor road?

7 Name two French airlines. One is an international operation. The other operates inside France.

8 What is a traffic policeman called in French?

9 At the port you may have seen a warning against bringing animals into Britain because of the danger of spreading the disease rabies. What is the French for rabies?

10 Complete the following French road sign
PRIORITÉ À ?

Extra Extra Extra Extra Extra

☆ What would be the advantages or disadvantages of changing from miles to kilometres in Britain?

☆ Should the British change to driving on the right-hand side of the road? Why or why not?

☆ Copy or trace this outline map of France into your note book. Put in as many towns, rivers, mountains and seas as you can.

☆ Consider the advantages of a common European system of road signs. How easy or difficult would this be to put into practice?

Answers to quiz

C-route communale	Marchandises à déclarer	On the back of a lorry
The green sticker	Blue	Air Inter Air France
Droite	La rage	Un car
		Un motard

Bon appétit

You'll have seen lots of adverts for restaurants like these when you were **On the spot.** Now you're back see if you can work out the answers to these questions using the adverts on this page.

1 Which of these restaurants are near the sea?

2 How can you tell?

3 In which of these places could you stay the night? Which words tell you this?

4 Which restaurant specialises in sea food?

5 Give the names of 2 *fruits de mer*.

6 In which region do you find the largest number of crêperies?

7 *Couscous* is a north African speciality made from maize. This couscous shop has a restaurant and a take-away service. What is the French for take-away?

Extra Extra Extra Extra Extra Extra

1 Which British dishes would you have liked to have seen on French menus?

2 Which French dishes would you like to see on menus here?

3 What were your favourite foods in France? Make up a menu using all the foods you particularly liked in France.

4 Make up an advert in French for a restaurant by the sea. Use the adverts on these pages to help you.

5 Here's a recipe for *crêpes*. But the instructions have been jumbled up. Put them in the right order and write out the recipe correctly. If you tried any crêpes in France, write down the flavours of those you tasted.
** *Bien mélanger et battre le tout.*
** *Cuire à feu modéré.*
** *Ajoutez 3 oeufs, 20g de beurre, du sel et ¼ litre de lait.*
** *Mettre 500g de farine dans un bol.*
** *Laisser reposer 45 minutes.*

Food in the Shops

What does this shop sell?

List as many French food shops as you can. Here are some names which need to be finished off.

p â t _ _ _ _ _ _ _
c h a r _ _ _ _ _ _ _
b o u c _ _ _ _ _
b o u _ _ _ _ _ _
c h e _ _ _ _ _ _
é p i _ _ _ _ _
p o i s s _ _ _ _ _ _ _
a l i m e _ _ _ _ _ _ _
b o u l _ _ _ _ _ _ _

Pardon, monsieur!

Aïe! Mes pâtisseries!

Around the town

The photo on the right shows firemen at work in France.

– In which town is it?
– What is the French for fireman?
– What does the shop shown in the photo sell?
– Who was Gambetta?
– A speciality of this area of France is a dish called **tripes à la mode de ?** Give the name of the town.
– What does '*Au secours!*' mean?

Gambetta is mentioned on the left too.
– In which town was this photo taken?
– What is Orly?
– RATP stands for **Régie**

Autonome des Transports Parisiens.
Name one other means of transport on which you can see these letters.
(Answers on page 96)

Extra Extra Extra Extra

Distinguished French people are remembered on street names, bank notes and in the names of schools. Are famous British celebrities honoured in the same way? What sorts of people are remembered in the names of streets or schools or on bank notes here?

Louis Pasteur (1822-1895) a most important French bacteriologist, is famous for discoveries in the treatment of contagious diseases and for the purification of milk. He devised a method of purifying milk by heating it to a certain temperature – pasteurisation.

Pasteur also discovered how to protect sheep and cattle from the deadly disease of anthrax by injecting them with some of the weakened germs of the disease itself – the principle of vaccination.

RUE PASTEUR

He extended this method to the treatment of rabies. He also discovered and overcame the germ which was destroying the silk worms of France and threatening the entire silk industry.

Much of Pasteur's most important work was completed in the years following a major stroke. His illness affected one half of his brain and yet he was still able to continue with his work!

Mystery photos

The photographs show some things you may have seen **Around the Town** in France. But they aren't complete. Can you work out what they are?

The answers are jumbled up at the bottom of the page in case you get stuck.

Extra Extra Extra Extra Extra Extra

PLACE PIERRE ET MARIE CURIE
(1859-1906)
(1867-1934)

Pierre, a physicist, together with his wife made the important discovery of the metallic element **Radium** now used in the treatment of cancer. Their name is used to describe a unit of radioactivity, a **Curie**.

AVENUE VICTOR HUGO
(1802-1885)

A writer, best known as the leader of the Romantic movement in French literature. His most famous works include *Les Misérables* (novel), *Les Contemplations* (poems), *Notre-Dame de Paris* (historical novel).

RUE MARÉCHAL FOCH
(1851-1929)

Famous for his part in the battle of the Somme during the first world war.

Answers

A French bus; A bus stop; Tabac sign; Gendarmerie sign; A Citroën 2CV car; The Eiffel Tower and the river Seine; A sign post pointing to QUAIS RIVE GAUCHE, TOUR EIFFEL, PONT DES INVALIDES

Signs and adverts

This poster is warning of the dangers of rabies, a dangerous, fatal disease. Rabies is widespread in France, but has not reached Britain. You are likely to see rabies notices at your port.

1 Why there?
2 How is the disease carried?
3 The disease is fatal to man unless precautions are taken. It was a Frenchman, a famous bacteriologist, who first discovered an antidote to rabies. He is often named on street signs and shown on postage stamps. Who is he?
4 Animals must not be brought into Britain unless they undergo a period of quarantine. Why is this?
5 Which domestic animals are affected by rabies?

Le **renard** est l'agent de diffusion de cette maladie. Par son intermédiare, certains animaux sauvages…et certains animaux domestiques notamment: Chats, Chiens et Bovins ont été atteints par la rage. Le virus de la rage est contenu dans le *cerveau* et la *salive* de l'animal malade.
Il peut ainsi être transmis à un autre animal ou à l'homme *par morsure* ou dépôt de salive virulente sur une plaie.

Abbreviations

You may have seen some of these abbreviations when you were in France. What do they stand for and where would you see them? Some of the more difficult ones have clues in brackets after them!

1 Kg 2 Km 3 g 4 RATP (travel) 5 SNCF 6 BD (newsagents) 7 PTT (circular sign outside)
8 CES ("We don't need no ? ") 9 RSVP (invitation) 10 AC (wine)

Answers on page 96

In which region of France is this food shop?

What are you encouraged to buy?

Is this an effective form of advertising?

How is the trout sold?

Name as many of the foods chalked on the blackboard as you can in English.

The town of **Niort** is mentioned in 2 of the adverts below. It's in the west of France near La Rochelle.

1 How can you tell from the adverts that **Niort** is on a river?

2 The **Auberge des Voyageurs** is in **Beauvoir,** 17km from Niort. It is closed for one day during each week. Which day is it?

3 When are the annual holidays at the Auberge?

4 Write down the French for weekly and yearly.

The windmill advert is encouraging you to visit a windmill in the département of Vendée in Western France.

1 How long do they claim that the windmill has been turning?

2 You can only visit the windmill at certain times. What are they?

3 If you were to go along in July, would you be able to see it?

4 What do they sell there especially for the tourists?

Let's Go Shopping

Which go together? Match the price labels to the goods on the market stalls.

4.90 F
le paquet

5F
La bouteille

55F.
la paire

6.50F
la boîte

6F
le Kg.

5F
les 200g

10F
la pièce

7.50F
la douzaine

30F
le mètre

10F
la livre

Compare Prices

Are these things more or less expensive in France? Write down the approximate prices in France and Britain.

une baguette
un café-crème
une glace – un cornet à une boule
un verre de limonade dans un café
une bouteille de limonade dans un supermarché

un magazine de mode
une carte postale
une tablette de chocolat (100g)
du chewing-gum

Extra Extra

— Did the rate of exchange vary while you were in France?

— Where did you change your money back into sterling?

— Write a list of 6 inexpensive things which you would advise people to buy in France as typically French souvenirs.

True or False?

Look at these pictures. they will help you decide whether the sentences below are true or false.

1 A *poissonnerie* is a place where fish is sold.
2 *Bénodet* is a town in Normandy.
3 Madame Bodivit sells her fish from a mobile shop.
4 She parks it near the river.
5 Mobile shops in France are usually made by *Citroën*.

PARKING MAIRIE
BÉNODET
POISSONNERIE
VENTE EN CAMION MAGASIN
CHOIX · QUALITÉ · PRIX
Madame Yvonne BODIVIT   Tél. 91.04.80
N° SIR 780 106 951 00012

1 *Le Moussaillon* (The Ship's Boy) sells windsurfing boards.
2 You can rent windsurfing boards from there.
3 The shop only sells *children's* clothes.
4 It is situated in an industrial zone.
5 It is closed on Mondays.

LE MOUSSAILLON   Le Spécialiste du Vêtement de Mer
CIRES COTTEN
de Loisirs :
Blousons
Pulls
Jean's Lee Cooper
Location et Vente de Planches à Voile
Z. I. du Moros   -   Ouvert tous les jours
Parking assuré

Money Quiz

1 Which coin has a map of France on one side?
a. 0.20F   **b.** 1F   **c.** 0.50F   **d.** 10F
2 Here are the names of the men shown on French bank notes. Which go with which notes?
The composer, Berlioz
The Painter, La Tour
The writer, Pascal
The painter, Delacroix
3 How many centimes are there in 1 franc?
a. 1,000   **b.** 100   **c.** 10   **d.** 20
4 On which coins or notes is the symbolic figure called *la semeuse*?
10F   500F   0.50F   5F   2F   1F
5 Which of these words are shown on French *coins*? What do they mean?
*Liberté Banque Fraternité Caissier
République Egalité*
Answers, page 96

At the café

True or Flase?

1 *Service Compris* written on a bill means you don't have to leave a tip.
2 *Une bière à la pression* is bottled beer.
3 *Taxe sur la Valeur Ajoutée* (TVA) is the equivalent of our VAT.
4 The liqueur, *Bénédictine,* is made in Normandy.
5 French sandwiches are smaller than British ones, and contain more butter.
6 French cafés are closed on Sundays.
7 *Vittel* is the name of a French mineral water.
8 You'll find *un babyfoot* in a café.
9 *Une menthe à l'eau* is coloured blue.
10 *Ricard* is the name of a brand of French cigarettes.

Answers, page 96

Benedictine works, Fécamp

BOISSONS PILOTES

CATEGORIE **B**

DÉSIGNATION DES BOISSONS		comptoir	salle et terrasse
CONTENANCE petit verre 12 à 15 cl grand verre 20 à 25 cl		1,30	2,30
CAFÉ	la tasse		
BIÈRE	le demi		
	ou 1/4 flacon	0,75	1,75
EAU MINÉRALE Vittel	petit verre	0,75	1,75
	grand verre	1,50	2,50
	ou 1/4 flacon		
LIMONADE	petit verre	0,75	1,85
	grand verre		
	ou 1/4 flacon		
BOISSONS aux FRUITS	petit verre	0,70	1,70
	grand verre	1,30	2,30
	ou 1/4 flacon		
LAIT	petit verre	0,70	1,70
	ou grand verre	1,40	2,40
SIROP DE : CITRON MENTHE GRENADINE	petit verre		
	ou grand verre		

PRIX SERVICE 15 % NON COMPRIS

How do the prices on this *Boissons Pilotes* compare to those in France when you were there?

If you order 1 coffee, 1 small glass of milk and 1 small glass of lemonade at the bar of this café, how much will you have to pay?

Is service included?

Which of these drinks could you have ordered in France?

Sirop   Pernod   Pschitt   Orangina
Menthe à l'eau   Byrrh   Cognac   Martini
Citron pressé   Bière   Cidre   Choky   Gini

If you were in a *café-tabac* what would you be able to buy apart from drinks?

Café crossword

Clues

Across

1 Café serving food
4 prix _ _ t
6 _ _ _ _ _ _ _ _ Pilotes
7 It's cheaper _ _ comptoir
8 A cheese sandwich - un sandwich au ?
10 Café, 1F50 _ _ tasse
11 An orange juice - un jus d' _ _ _ _ _ _
13 Quel âge as-tu? J'ai 18 _ _ _
14 L'alcool _ _ sera pas servi aux mineurs.
16 Let's listen to the _ _ _ _ _ _ _ _

Down

1 Football at the café
2 Service en _ _ _
3 To clean your fingers use a _ _ _ _ _ _ -doigts
5 De l' _ _ _ minérale
7 Pineapple
9 Green drink _ une _ _ _ _ _ _ _ à l'eau
10 Same as 10 across
12 Service _ _ sus
15 Un _ _ s de fruits

Solution, page 96

93

Enjoy yourself

Enjoy yourself?
Well, I hope you did?

Think about some of the things
you enjoyed most.
Look at these adverts.
Did *you* go to
un cinéma   une piscine?   une discothèque?
un son et lumière?   un château?
Is there any particular thing which will remind you of
France? Which record did you hear most often? Was it
French, American or British?

VERSAiLLES (78). Château et musée.
950.58.32. Tlj sf Lun et jours fériés de 9h45 à
17h30. Entrée : 9 F. Dim et jours fériés : 4,50 F.
(Fermeture des caisses à 16 h 30). Grands appartements et galerie des glaces, visite libre. Visites
commentées des appartements privés et de l'Opéra
Royal. Billets spéciaux et départ dans le second
vestibule. Visites en anglais et en allemand. **Grand
Trianon,** Tlj sf Lun de 9h45 à 17h. (Fermeture des
caisses à 16h30). **Petit Trianon** Tlj sf Sam, Dim,
Lun de 14h à 17h. Visite du Parc : 6 F. — 10 ans
gratuit. **Inauguration Chambre du Roi et de la
galerie des Glaces.** Uniquement par groupe de 30
personnes. Tlj sf Lun de 9h45 à 17h30. **Grandes
eaux** de 16h à 17h30, les 14 et 21 sept. **Fêtes de
nuit** les 13 et 14 septembre, à 21h.

son & lumière

HOTEL NATIONAL DES INVALIDES. Cour d'hon-
neur (M° Invalides). Rens. 979.00.15. « Ombres de
gloire », textes d'André Castelot, musique de Georges Delerue, mise en scène de Pierre Arnaud.
Version française à 22h30. Version anglaise à
21h30 et 23h15. Entrée : 18 F. Enf — 12 ans :
14 F. Prix pour groupes. (Jusqu'au 12 octobre).

Au Bœuf sur le Toit

19, rue d'Abbeville
80000 AMIENS

ouvert tous les jours
jusqu'à 3 h. du matin   (lundi)

*son restaurant
*son bar *son cabaret
*sa discothèque

PISCINE DELIGNY 25, quai A.-France
Pt Concorde 551.72.15
La plage de Paris - 3000 m² de solarium
Alimentée en eau potab. - Bar.-rest. - ouv. m. et s.
BATEAU ECOLE tte l'année - Permis mer et riv.

Cars Cars Cars Cars

Finish

T	O	E	E	P
T	C	G	U	A
L	I	T	M	C
U	A	R	I	S
E	N	O	Ë	N
R				

Start

These photos show
models of the big four
makes of car you saw
in France. What are
those makes?
Their names are
spelled out somewhere
in this puzzle. Start at
the letter **R**. You can
move up or down, or
across, but not
diagonally.

en version originale système Dolby **MARIGNAN PATHE** · **UGC NORMANDIE** ·
en version française son stéréophonique 70 mm **LE GRAND REX**
en version originale **UGC ODEON**
en version française son stéréophonique **WEPLER PATHE** - **CONVENTION GAUMONT**
en version française **GAUMONT SUD** - **GAUMONT GAMBETTA** - **UGC GOBELINS** - **GAUMONT HALLES**
UGC Gare de Lyon - **3 MURAT** - **GAUMONT BERLITZ** - **MONTPARNASSE PATHE**

LA GUERRE DES ETOILES CONTINUE...
STAR WARS
L'EMPIRE CONTRE-ATTAQUE

Horoscope in France!

(ne prenez pas au sérieux!) Quelle est la date de votre anniversaire? Et quel est votre signe du zodiaque?

Bélier (21 mars – 20 avril)
Faites attention en classe! Vous êtes sérieux et prudent. Une période attentive dans votre vie.

Balance (24 septembre – 23 octobre)
Ne perdez pas de poids. Ne balancez pas! Prenez des décisions définitives!

Taureau (21 avril – 20 mai)
Attention aux vaches! Attendez votre revanche! Attaquez vos projets sérieusement!

Scorpion (24 octobre – 22 novembre)
Ne travaillez pas trop! Gardez les pieds sur terre!

Gémeaux (21 mai – 21 juin)
Période calme et tranquille! Rentrée d'argent!

Sagittaire (23 novembre – 21 décembre)
Amusez-vous bien! Ne travaillez pas trop!

Cancer (22 juin – 22 juillet)
Voyage au bord de la mer! Attention en traversant la rue!

Capricorne (22 décembre – 20 janvier)
Fuyez les taureaux! Soyez prudent!

Lion (23 juillet – 23 août)
Une période heureuse pour les sportifs! Mais écoutez les conseils!

Verseau (21 janvier – 18 février)
Soyez gentil avec vos professeurs! Evitez les accidents!

Vierge (24 août – 23 septembre)
Soyez prudent toute l'année. Faites confiance aux poissons.

Poissons (19 février – 20 mars)
Evitez la pêche! Période calme dans votre vie.

We've got *nearly* all the answers!

Page 6: Quiz

1c 2a 3c 4a 5b 6c
7c 8b 9a,b,d 10c
11c 12c 13b 14c
15b 16a.

Page 86: Photo questions

photo 1
— The firemen are in Deauville on the Normandy coast
— Un pompier
— Meat
— French lawyer and politician
— Tripes à la mode de Caen
— Help!

photo 2
— The photo was taken in Paris
— One of Paris's airports
— A metro train

Page 89: Abbreviations

1 Kilo 2 Kilomètre 3 Gramme
4 Régie Autonome des Transports Parisiens – Buses and metro in Paris
5 Société Nationale des Chemins de Fer Français – French Railways
6 Bande Dessinée – comic strip
7 Postes et Télécommunications
8 Collège d'Enseignement Secondaire – secondary school
9 Répondez, s'il vous plaît
10 Appellation Contrôlée – on wine bottles

Page 90: Money Quiz

1,d **2,** 500F – Pascal, 100F – Delacroix, 50F – La Tour 10F – Berlioz **3,**b **4,** 5F, 2F, 1F, 0.50F **5,** Liberté (freedom), Egalité (equality), Fraternité (brotherhood), République (Republic)

Page 92: True or False?

1 True, it means service included
2 False, it's draught beer
3 True
4 True, it's made in Fécamp in Normandy
5 False, French sandwiches contain no butter and are large.
6 False
7 True
8 True, it's a café football machine
9 False, it's a green drink
10 False, it's the name of an apéritif, an aniseed-flavoured drink.

Page 93: Café Crossword

Across 1 brasserie **4** net **6** boissons **7** au
8 fromage **10** la **11** orange **13** ans **14** ne
16 juke-box

Down 1 babyfoot **2** sus **3** rince **5** eau **7** ananas
9 menthe **10** la **12** en **15** ju

L'Hymne National Français

La Marseillaise is a song of war. The words and music were written by *Rouget de Lisle* in 1792 when he was a young officer garrisoned in Strasbourg. After letting the mayor of Strasbourg hear his song, Rouget de Lisle soon found that the whole of Strasbourg was taken by it. It soon spread as far as Marseille, and the first soldiers to bring the song to Paris were in fact soldiers from Marseille, *les Marseillais*. *La chanson des Marseillais* soon became known as *La Marseillaise*, one of the most rousing of national anthems.

First Verse
Allons, enfants de la patrie,
Le jour de gloire est arrivé!
Contre nous de la tyrannie
L'étendard sanglant est levé!
L'étendard sanglant est levé!
Entendez-vous dans les campagnes
Mugir ces féroces soldats?
Ils viennent jusque dans nos bras,
Egorgez vos fils, vos compagnes.

Refrain
Aux armes, citoyens!
Formez vos bataillons!
Marchons, marchons,
Qu'un sang impur
Abreuve nos sillons!